T0205775

Communications in Computer and Information Science   **1317**

More information about this series at http://www.springer.com/series/7899

Ripon Patgiri · Sivaji Bandyopadhyay ·
Malaya Dutta Borah ·
Dalton Meitei Thounaojam (Eds.)

Big Data,
Machine Learning,
and Applications

First International Conference, BigDML 2019
Silchar, India, December 16–19, 2019
Revised Selected Papers

 Springer

Editors
Ripon Patgiri 🆔
National Institute of Technology Silchar
Silchar, India

Sivaji Bandyopadhyay
National Institute of Technology Silchar
Silchar, India

Malaya Dutta Borah
National Institute of Technology Silchar
Silchar, India

Dalton Meitei Thounaojam
National Institute of Technology Silchar
Silchar, India

ISSN 1865-0929   ISSN 1865-0937 (electronic)
Communications in Computer and Information Science
ISBN 978-3-030-62624-2   ISBN 978-3-030-62625-9 (eBook)
https://doi.org/10.1007/978-3-030-62625-9

This Springer imprint is published by the registered company Springer Nature Switzerland AG
The registered company address is: Gewerbestrasse 11, 6330 Cham, Switzerland

Preface

The National Institute of Technology, Silchar, India, organized the International Conference on Big Data, Machine Learning, and Applications (BigDML 2019) during December 16–19, 2019. BigDML 2019 is a premier annual international forum for big data and machine learning researchers, scientists, practitioners, application developers, and users. The BigDML conference aims to bring together researchers around the world to exchange research results and address open issues in all aspects of big data and machine learning. BigDML 2019 is an outstanding platform to discuss the key findings, exchange novel ideas, listening to world class leaders, and share experiences with peer groups. The conference provides the opportunities for collaboration with national and international organizations of repute to the research community. BigDML 2019 witnessed a large number of participants and submissions from around the world.

BigDML 2019 was organized in order to consider unpublished original research works in big data and machine learning. There were 152 papers submitted of which 32 were accepted. These conference proceedings contain 9 papers out of 32 accepted papers. Apart from the 32 accepted and presented papers, 6 internationally renowned speakers like Padma Shri Prof. Ajay Kumar Ray, Prof. Alexander Gelbukh, Prof. Punam Kumar Saha, Prof. Paolo Rosso, Prof. Jossef Van Genabith, and Prof. Alain Tremeau shared their experience with the participants. These conference proceedings are able to disseminate high-quality research results in the relevant fields.

October 2020

Ripon Patgiri
Sivaji Bandyopadhyay
Malaya Dutta Borah
Dalton Meitei Thounaojam

Organization

Advisory Committee

Rajkumar Buyya	The University of Melbourne, Australia
Padma Shri Ajay Kumar Ray	Indian Institute of Technology Kharagpur, India
Pushpak Bhattacharyya	Indian Institute of Technology Bombay, India
Kalyanmoy Deb	Michigan State University, USA
Narasimhan Sundarajan	Nanyang Technological University, Singapore
Francisco Herrera	University of Granada, Spain
V. Ramachandran	Anna University, India
Marina L. Gavrilova	University of Calgary, Canada
Vincenzo Piuri	University of Milan, Italy
Janusz Kacprzyk	Polish Academy of Sciences, Poland
Alexander Gelbukh	Instituto Politécnico Nacional, Mexico
Rainer Malaka	Universität Bremen, Germany
Monojit Choudhury	Microsoft Research Lab, India
Alain Tremeau	Université Jean Monnet, France
Timothy A. Gonsalves	Indian Institute of Technology Mandi, India

Organizing Committee

Chief Patron

Sivaji Bandyopadhyay	NIT Silchar, India

Patron

Samir Kumar Borgohain	NIT Silchar, India

General Chairs

Sivaji Bandyopadhyay	NIT Silchar, India
Ripon Patgiri	NIT Silchar, India

Organizing Chairs

Dalton Meitei Thounaojam	NIT Silchar, India
Malaya Dutta Borah	NIT Silchar, India

Program Chairs

Thoudam Doren Singh	NIT Silchar, India
Anupam Biswas	NIT Silchar, India

Publicity Chairs

Partha Pakray	NIT Silchar, India
Suganya Devi K.	NIT Silchar, India

Finance and Hospitality Chairs

Anish Kumar Saha	NIT Silchar, India
Laiphrakpam Dolendro Singh	NIT Silchar, India

Award Chairs

Sanasam Ranbir Singh	IIT Guwahati, India
Bhaskar Biswas	IIT (BHU) Varanasi, India
Sandip Chkroborty	IIT Kharagpur, India

Committee Members

Biswajit Purakayashtha	NIT Silchar, India
Ujwala Baruah	NIT Silchar, India
Samir Kumar Borgohain	NIT Silchar, India
Pinki Roy	NIT Silchar, India
Biswanath Dey	NIT Silchar, India
P. S. Neog	NIT Silchar, India
Pantha Kanti Nath	NIT Silchar, India
Saroj Kumar Biswas	NIT Silchar, India
Badal Soni	NIT Silchar, India
Umakanta Majhi	NIT Silchar, India
Shyamosree Pal	NIT Silchar, India
Shyamapada Mukherjee	NIT Silchar, India

Technical Program Committee

Rainer Unland	University of Duisburg-Essen, Germany
Annappa	NITK Surathkal, India
Heder Soares Bernardino	Federal University of Juiz de Fora, Brazil
Atul Negi	University of Hyderabad, India
Huiru (Jane) Zheng	Ulster University, UK
C. T. Bhunia	NIT Arunachal Pradesh, India
Subhash Saini	NASA, USA
Rajni Jindal	DTU Delhi, India
Parimala Thulasiraman	University of Manitoba, Canada
Daya Gupta	DTU Delhi, India
Valentina Emilia Balas	Automation and Applied Informatics, Aurel Vlaicu University of Arad, Romania
Parimala N.	JNU Delhi, India
Sung-Bae Cho	Yonsei University, South Korea

Pradip Kumar Das	Indian Institute of Technology Guwahati, India
David Eduardo Pinto Avendaña	Benemérita Universidad Autónoma de Puebla, Mexico
R. K. Agrawal	Jawaharlal Nehru University, India
Grigori Sidorov	Instituto Politécnico Nacional (IPN), Mexico
Nidul Sinha	National Institute of Technology, Silchar, India
Rabiah Abdul Kadir	Universiti Kebangsaan Malaysia, Malaysia
Sudipta Roy	Assam University, India
Rabiah Ahmad	Universiti Teknikal Malaysia, Malaysia
Ganesh Chandra Deka	Ministry of Skill Development and Entrepreneurship, Government of India, India
Dibyajyoti Dutta	Ministry of Development of Northeastern region, NIC Delhi, India
Sumit Jaiswal	Ministry of Electronics & IT (MeitY), India
Yumnam Jayanta	NIELIT Kolkata, India
Khumanthem Manglem Singh	NIT Manipur, India
K. Vivekanandan	Pondicherry Engineering College, India
S. M. Warusia Mohamed S. M. M. Yassin	Universiti Teknikal Malaysia, Malaysia
Shahin Ara Begum	Assam University, India
Tandra Pal	NIT Durgapur, India
Moumita Roy	IIIT Guwahati, India
Suchetana Chakraborty	IIIT Guwahati, India
Vijay Bhaskar Semwal	NIT Rourkela, India
Sontosh Kumar	IIIT Nayaraipur, India
Durgesh Singh	BITS Mesra, India
Debasis Das	BITS Pilani, India
Jims Marchang	Sheffield Hallam University, UK
Sudip Kumar Naskar	Jadavpur University, India
Kishorjit Nongmeikapam	Indian Institute of Information Technology Manipur, India
Prem Nath	Mizoram University, India
Swarup Roy	Sikkim University, India
Arnab Maji	North-Eastern Hill University, India
Rajiv Misra	Indian Institute of Technology Patna, India
Somnath Mukhopadhyay	Assam University Silchar, India
Santanu Pal	Universität des Saarlandes, Germany
Braja Gopal Patra	The University of Texas Health Science Center, USA
Anand Kumar M.	National Institute of Technology Karnataka, Surathkal, India
Dipankar Das	Jadavpur University, India
Elena Yagunova	Saint Petersburg State University, Russia
Utpal Sharma	Tezpur University, India
Khin Mar Soe	University of Computer Studies, Yangon, Myanmar
Shirshendu Das	IIT Ropar, India

Contents

TUKNN: A Parallel KNN Algorithm to Handle Large Data

Parthajit Borah[✉], Aguru Teja, Saurabh Anand Jha, and Dhruba K. Bhattacharyya

Department of Computer Science, Tezpur University, Tezpur, Assam, India
parthajit@tezu.ernet.in

Abstract. In this work, we study the performance of the K-Nearest Neighbour (KNN) based predictive model in sequential as well as parallel mode to observe its performance both in terms of accuracy and execution time. We propose a parallel KNN algorithm, called TUKNN to handle voluminous data. Based on our experimental study, it has been observed that our method is capable of handling datasets with large dimensionality and instances with high accuracy. We also recommend best possible proximity measure and optimal range of K values for better accuracy.

Keywords: Supervised · Feature · Parallel · Classification · Optimal

1 Introduction

With the proliferation of data being generated, there is an urgent need of new technologies and architectures to make possible to extract valuable information from it by capturing and analysis process. New sources of data include various sensor enabled devices like medical devices, IP cameras, video surveillance cameras, and set-top boxes, which contribute largely to the volume of big data. Due to data proliferation, it is predicted that 44 zettabytes or 44 trillion gigabytes of data will be generated annually by the end of 2020[1]. The data are continuously generated by the sources from internet applications and communications which are of large size, different variety, structured or unstructured, which is referred to as Big data. Big Data is characterized by three particularly significant V's -Volume, Velocity, and Variety. The term Volume signifies the plethora of data produced from time to time by various different organizations and institutes. Velocity characterizes the rate at which data is generated from different sources. The third V, Variety denotes the diverse forms of data which may be structured, semi-structured or unstructured, generated from several organizations. For example, data can be in the form of video, image, text, audio, etc. Apart from the mentioned characteristics above, two other key features are–incremental and dispersed nature. They are incremental in the sense that there is dynamic addition of new incoming data to the pile of big data. Big data are dispersed in nature because they are geographically distributed across different data centers. These are some of the distinguishing characteristics which sets big data apart from traditional

---

[1] https://www.emc.com/leadership/digital-universe/2014iview/index.htm.

© Springer Nature Switzerland AG 2020
R. Patgiri et al. (Eds.): BigDML 2019, CCIS 1317, pp. 1–13, 2020.
https://doi.org/10.1007/978-3-030-62625-9_1

databases or data-warehouses. The traditional data storage techniques are not adequate to store and analyze those huge volume of data. In short, such a data is so large and complex that most traditional data management tools are inadequate to store or process it efficiently.

There are various challenges associated with big data. Such a large volume of data if processed sequentially it takes lot of time. Second, how do we process and extract valuable information from the huge volume of data within the given timeframe? To address the challenges, it is required to know various computational complexities, information security, and computational method, to analyze big data. For example, many statistical methods that perform well for small data size do not scale to voluminous data. Similarly, many computational techniques that perform well for small data face significant challenges in analyzing big data. Big data analytics is the use of advanced analytic techniques against very large, diverse data sets that include structured, semi-structured and unstructured data, from different sources, and in different sizes from terabytes to zettabytes.

Predictive analysis gives a list of solutions by establishing the previous data patterns for a given situation. It studies the present as well as the past data and predict what may happen in the future or gives the probability what would happen in the future. We need to make use of such large data in order to make decisions in future. However, traditional machine learning and statistical methods in sequential mode takes much longer time in order to make prediction, especially, in case of intrusion data [3]. In this work, a traditional machine learning model–KNN with various proximity measures is studied both in sequential and parallel manner.

The major contribution of this paper is a parallel version of the KNN algorithm referred here as TUKNN. We also conduct an exhaustive experimental study on a good number of proximity measures in the KNN framework and recommend the best possible measure to achieve best effective, better accuracy with TUKNN algorithm. Further, we also recommend an optimal range for 'k' values to achieve best possible performance.

2 Related Work

KNN is a non-parametric classification method, which is simple but effective in many cases [5]. It classifies objects based on the closest training example in the feature space. For any test object t which is to be classified, its K nearest neighbors are retrieved, and this forms the neighborhood of the object t. Then based on a majority voting among the neighbours, the class label of t is decided.

In [9], the authors use the CUDA (Compute Unified Device Architecture) thread model to implement a CUDA based KNN algorithm. Adult data from UCI Machine Learning Repository were used to compare the performance of CUDA based implementation on GPU with ordinary CPU based implementation and authors suggests that KNN method is efficient for applications with large volume of data.

In [8], the authors implement CUKNN algorithm which constructs two multi- thread kernels such as distance calculation kernel and sorting kernel. With CUKNN, the authors claims that the method could achieve 15.2 times better execution time performance than CPU.

In [2], the authors propose a fast and parallel KNN algorithm and show the impact on content-based image retrieval applications. The authors implement the parallel version of KNN in C and MATLAB using GPU with CUDA.

3   Proposed Work

KNN is a widely used classification algorithm and can be considered parallel friendly because of the number of independent operations. When the training and testing datasets are large, then the speed of execution becomes quite slow which makes it suitable for parallel implementation. In this work, we implement KNN on CUDA framework. The proposed framework is depicted in Fig. 1. In our framework, we explore a good no of proximity measures in parallel during the mining process to recommend the best possible measure for better accuracy. The measures used are: Euclidean distance, Manhattan distance, Kulczynski distance, cosine similarity, Chebyshev Distance, Soergel distance, Sorensen, and Tanimoto.

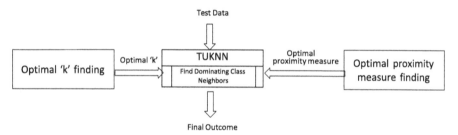

Fig. 1. Framework of the proposed work

3.1   Distance Measures

Dissimilarity is an essential component in the KNN algorithm. It influences the performance of the algorithm significantly in terms of speed and accuracy. Since, every proximity (similarity or dissimilarity) measure has its own advantages and disadvantages. So, we conduct an empirical study to evaluate their performance and subsequently to recommend the best possible measure for cost effective performance with TUKNN. Table 1 shows the distance measures and their mathematical expressions used in our work.

Further, we also carry out an exhaustive experimentation on large no of datasets by varying the K values to identify an optimal range of K values for best possible performance by TUKNN. Next, we present both sequential and parallel version of KNN algorithm.

3.2   Sequential KNN Algorithm

[1]   For every fold in the 5 folds perform the steps 2 to 8.

Table 1. Distance measures and their mathematical expressions [4, 11]

Measure & References	Math Expression
Euclidean	$D_{xy} = \sqrt{(\sum_{i=1}^{m}(x_i - y_i)^2)}$
Manhattan	$D_{Manhattan}(x, y) = \|x_i - y_i\|$
Kulczynski	$D_{kulczynski}(x, y) = \dfrac{(\sum \|x_i - y_i\|)}{(\sum max(x_i, y_i))}$
Chebyshev	$D_{Chebyshev}(x, y) = max_i(\|x_i - y_i\|)$
Cosine	$Sim(A, B) = cos(\theta) = \dfrac{A.B}{\|\|A\|\|\|\|B\|\|}$
Sorgel	$D_{sg} = \dfrac{\sum_{i=1}^{d}\|P_i - Q_i\|}{\sum_{i=1}^{d} min(P_i, Q_i)}$
Sorenson	$D_{soresnosn} = \dfrac{2\|x.y\|}{\|x\|^2 + \|y\|^2}$
Tanimoto	$D_{tanimoto} = \dfrac{x.y}{\|x\|*\|x\| + \|y\|*\|y\| - x.y}$

[2] Split the dataset into test set and training set using 5-fold cross validation.

[3] For every test instance in the test set perform the steps 4 to 8.

[4] Find the distance between this test instance and all the training instances in the training set.

[5] Now, from the distances obtained from the step 4, find the first maximum K number of minimum values and thereby save the respective training instances having those values. Here, the maximum K value in the range (of K values) is chosen for the algorithm.

[6] For every K in a range of values perform the steps 7 & 8.

[7] Find the first K neighbors (i.e. the first K training instances with the minimum distances) from the results obtained in the step 5.

[8] Perform a majority voting among these neighbors; the dominating class label in the pool will become the class label of the test instance.

In step 5, instead of applying a sorting algorithm, we find the first K minimum distances and their respective training instances. This has been done in order to decrease the time complexity of the algorithm as the best sorting algorithm (Quick sort) takes $O(N^2)$ time where finding the first K minimum distances takes $O(NK_{max})$ time. Here, N represents the size of the input (training set) and K_{max} is the maximum K-Value in a range chosen for the algorithm.

3.3 The Proposed Parallel KNN Algorithm

The algorithm for parallel KNN implementation is stated below.

[1] For every fold in the 5 folds perform the steps 2 to 8.

[2] Split the dataset into test set and training set using 5-fold cross validation.

[3] For every n instances (2500) in the test set, perform the steps 4 to 8.

[4] Compute the distances between these n instances and all the training instances in the training set simultaneously by invoking the GPU kernel.

[5] Now, from the distances obtained from the step 4, find the first maximum K number of minimum values and thereby save the respective training instances having those values. The maximum K is the maximum K value in the range of K values chosen for the algorithm. This step is performed for all these n instances simultaneously with the help of the GPU kernel.

[6] For every K, perform the steps 7 & 8.

[7] Find the first K neighbors (i.e. the first K training instances with the minimum distances) from the results obtained in the step 5.

[8] Perform a majority voting among these neighbors and the dominating class label in the pool will become the class label of the test instance. The steps 6, 7 and 8 are performed for all these n instances simultaneously by invoking the GPU kernel.

4   Implementation and Results

For the parallel KNN, we compute all the distances between a set of test instances and all the training instances simultaneously. Hence, all the distances are computed in parallel at once. To calculate distance between the test instances and all the training instances in parallel, we use many cores of the GPU platform and develop the kernels in CUDA to compute the task in parallel. The most crucial task for a KNN classifier is to compute the distance d for finding the nearest neighbors. We implement the distance computation i.e. d on GPU platform which has resulted considerable improvement in the KNN performance.

The graphics card used in our work is NVIDIA Tesla k40c GPU Accelerator which has a memory of 12 GB. So, with a memory of 12 GB, we are able to compute the distance between 2500 test instances and all the training instances in the training set simultaneously on the GPU.

4.1   Datasets Used

We perform our experimentation on the following three types of datasets.

1. *Ransomware Dataset:* For our experiment, we use a dataset from Sgandurra et al. [10]. The dataset has total 582 and 942 instances of ransomware and goodware respectively. The 582 instances of ransomware comprise of 11 different variants. Also, it has total 30,692 features which collectively represent the characteristics of both goodware and ransomware. A detailed description of the dataset is given in the Table 2.

2. *SWaT Dataset:* Secure Water Treatment [1] (SWaT) data set is also used in our experimentation. The dataset contains a total of 946,722 instances out of which 54,620 instances belong to *attack* category. The dataset has 51 attributes and two labels namely *attack* and *normal*.

3. *UCI datasets:* A total of 20 datasets is also used in our work. The list of datasets used are given in the Table 3.

Table 2. Ransomware dataset characteristics

Sl no	Class	No of samples
1	Goodware	942
2	Critroni	50
3	CryptLocker	107
4	CryptoWall	46
5	KOLLAH	25
6	Kovter	64
7	Locker	97
8	MATSNU	59
9	PGPCODER	4
10	Reveton	90
11	TeslaCrypt	6
12	Trojan-Ransom	34
		Total samples: 1524
		Total features: 30962

4.2 Results and Observation

In our framework, an optimal range for K values is determined based on experimental study on twenty datasets from UCI Machine Learning repository. This testing reduces the overhead of calculating the best possible K values for highest accuracy and makes our model faster. As we can see form the Table 4, in the majority cases (15 out of 20) the results show optimal K values within the range of 2–9. Table 5 shows the ratio of CPU and GPU execution time for all the datasets used in our work. The optimal K value of each proximity measures for which highest accuracy is obtained is reported in Table 6, 7 and 8.

4.2.1 Accuracy Comparison

The graph plots for the accuracy comparison for three datasets are shown below.

1. *Accuracy of Binary Class Ransomware Dataset:* The classification accuracy of KNN algorithm with all the eight distance measures of ransomware dataset with binary class is shown in Fig. 2. As shown in the figure, the highest accuracy i.e., 95.27 is obtained with *Kulczynski, Soergel, Sorenson,* and *Tanimoto* measures.
2. *Accuracy of Multi Class Ransomware Dataset:* In this study, our observation from Fig. 3 is that 82.32 is the highest accuracy given by KNN with *Kulczynski* measure.

Table 3. Characteristics of 20 datasets obtained from UCI repository

S.I.	Dataset name	No of instances	No of features
1	Absenteeism at work	740	21
2	Audit	777	18
3	Banknote authentication	1372	5
4	Blood transfusion	748	5
5	Cardiotocography	2126	23
6	Diabetic debrecen	1151	20
7	Ecoli	336	8
8	Glass identification	214	10
9	Haberman	306	3
10	Hill valley	606	101
11	ILPD	583	10
12	Image segmentation	2310	19
13	Immunotherapy	90	8
14	Ionosphere	351	34
15	Iris	150	4
16	Libras	360	91
17	LSVT	126	309
18	Parkinson	756	754
19	Sonar	208	60
20	Soya bean	47	35

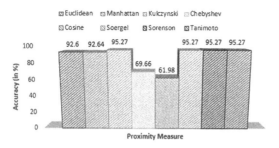

Fig. 2. Accuracy of ransomware dataset (binary class)

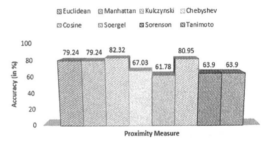

Fig. 3. Accuracy of ransomware dataset (multi class)

3. *Accuracy of SWaT Dataset:* Based on our study as depicted in Fig. 4 is that the model give same accuracy for all the eight measures i.e., 94.1 for this dataset. However, a difference in performance has been observed after *4th* decimal (not reported here).

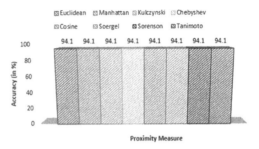

Fig. 4. Accuracy of SWaT dataset

4.2.2   Comparison of KNN and TUKNN in Terms of Execution Time

(a) *KNN vs TUKNN Time Comparison for Binary Ransomware Dataset:* The execution time comparison of KNN and TUKNN for binary ransomware dataset is shown in Fig. 5. It is clear from the figure that TUKNN performance is significantly better than KNN.

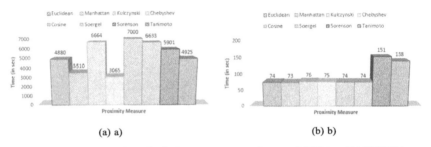

(a) a)   (b) b)

Fig. 5. Time comparison for 2-class ransomware dataset: a) KNN and b) TUKNN

Table 4. *K* values to achieve maximum accuracy

S.I.	Dataset name	No of instances	No of features	Value of K	Max Avg accuracy
1	Absenteeism at work	740	21	8	30.20%
2	Audit	777	18	3	93.70%
3	Banknote authentication	1372	5	4	100%
4	Blood transfusion	748	5	8	76.50%
5	Cardiotocography	2126	23	37	98.40%
6	Diabetic debrecen	1151	20	8	67.40%
7	Ecoli	336	8	8	79.00%
8	Glass identification	214	10	17	53.40%
9	Haberman	306	3	39	77.40%
10	Hill valley	606	101	3	54.70%
11	ILPD	583	10	49	70.90%
12	Image segmentation	2310	19	2	65.20%
13	Immunotherapy	90	8	5	78.60%
14	Ionosphere	351	34	3	83.20%
15	Iris	150	4	2	96.00%
16	Libras	360	91	3	11.50%
17	LSVT	126	309	50	65.90%
18	Parkinson	756	754	10	74.60%
19	Sonar	208	60	4	46.30%
20	Soya bean	47	35	2	98.00%

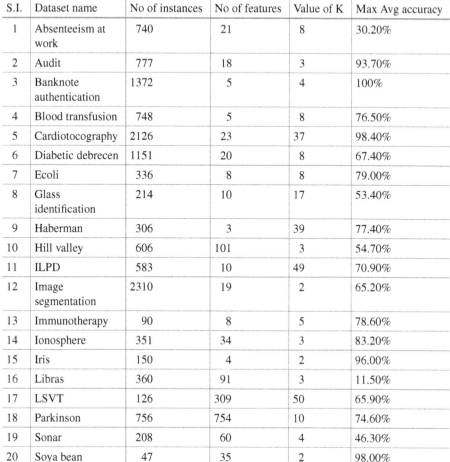

(a) c)   (b) d)

Fig. 6. Time comparison for multi-class ransomware dataset: c) KNN and d) TUKNN

(b) *KNN vs TUKNN Time Comparison for Multi-Class Ransomware Dataset:* Fig. 6
     shows the performance comparison of KNN and TUKNN for multi class ran-
     somware dataset. It is quite clear that TUKNN performance is much better than
     the KNN.
(c) *KNN vs TUKNN Time Comparison for SWaT Dataset:* In Fig. 7, it is clear that
     TUKNN implementation is significantly advantageous over KNN for SWaT dataset.

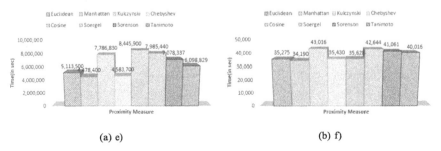

(a) e)   (b) f)

Fig. 7. Time comparison for SWaT dataset: e) KNN and f) TUKNN

Table 5. Ratio of CPU and GPU time (in seconds)

S. no	Proximity measures	Ransomware dataset		SWaT dataset
		Binary class	Multi class	Binary class
1	Euclidean distance	65.94	75.2	144.96
2	Manhattan distance	48.94	59.62	130.98
3	Chebyshev distance	40.86	50.19	129.37
4	Cosine similarity	94.59	100.9	237.05
5	Kulczynski distance	87.49	100.94	181.95
6	Soergel distance	89.63	104.06	187.25
7	Sorenson distance	39.07	42.95	172.38
8	Tanimoto distance	35.68	38.95	152.41
9	Motyka distance	70.91	77.21	193.68
10	Ruzicka distance	56.71	51.85	163

Table 6. Optimal 'K' values for proximity measures for 2-class ransomware dataset

Proximity measure	Optimal 'K' value	Accuracy
Euclidean	3	92.64
Manhattan	3	92.64
Kulczynski	3	95.27
Chebyshev	2	69.66
Cosine	7	61.9
Soergel	3	95.27
Sorenson	3	95.27
Tanimoto	3	95.27

Table 7. Optimal 'K' values for proximity measures for n-class ransomware dataset

Proximity measure	Optimal 'K' value	Accuracy
Euclidean	2	79.24
Manhattan	2	79.24
Kulczynski	3	82.32
Chebyshev	2	67.03
Cosine	8	61.78
Soergel	2	80.95
Sorenson	2	63.88
Tanimoto	2	63.88

Table 8. Optimal 'K' values for proximity measures for SWaT dataset

Proximity measure	Optimal 'K' value	Accuracy
Euclidean	9	94.08
Manhattan	9	94.08
Kulczynski	9	94.08
Chebyshev	9	94.08
Cosine	9	94.08
Soergel	9	94.08
Sorenson	9	94.08
Tanimoto	9	94.08

5   Conclusion

Our study reveals that Kulczynski distance and Soergel distance are adequate with KNN to handle 2-class ransomware dataset with high classification accuracy. However, in case of multi-class data handling, although these two proximity measures have been found to assist winning performance in comparison to its other counterparts, the classification accuracies are relatively less. Interestingly, for SWaT dataset, among eight proximity measures, six measures such as Euclidean, Manhattan, Kulczynski, Cosine Similarity, Chebyshev, and Soergel distance are giving equal winning performances.

Out of all the computations performed, the Chebyshev distance for the bi- nary classification of Ransomware Dataset is least benefitted from the usage of Py-CUDA where GPU computation is only 40.86 times faster than the CPU computation and the Cosine Similarity for the classification of SWaT Dataset is highly benefitted from the usage of Py-CUDA where the GPU computation is 237.5 times faster than the CPU computation.

When dealing with the binary classification of the Ransomware Dataset using the KNN model, if accuracy is of high priority, then usage of Kulczynski or Soergel Distance is recommended. Similarly, when dealing with the multi-class classification of the Ransomware Dataset, if accuracy is of high priority, then usage of Kulczynski Distance is recommended. When dealing with the classification of the SWaT Dataset with high accuracy, usage of any of these six proximity measures is recommended. But if both the accuracy and the computational time are of high priority, then the usage of the Manhattan Distance is a better option to go with.

Also, we recommend K values ranging from 2 to 9 for best possible accuracy for all the datasets used in the study. An exhaustive experimentation was also carried out for optimal feature selection based on some prominent feature selection algorithms [6, 7]. The performance of TUKNN with the optimal feature subset has been found significantly better than the present performance. However, due to lack of space, those results are not reported.

References

1. Secure Water Treatment (SWaT) Dataset (2018). https://itrust.sutd.edu.sg/itrust-labsdatasets/ datasetinfo/. Accessed 19 Dec 2018
2. Garcia, V., Debreuve, E., Barlaud, M.: Fast k nearest neighbor search using GPU. In: 2008 IEEE Computer Society Conference on Computer Vision and Pattern Recognition Workshops, pp. 1–6, June 2008. https://doi.org/10.1109/CVPRW.2008.4563100
3. Gogoi, P., Borah, B., Bhattacharyya, D.K.: Network anomaly identification using supervised classifier. Informatica 37(1) (2013)
4. Han, J., Kamber, M., Pei, J.: Data Mining: Concepts and Techniques, 3rd edn. Morgan Kaufmann Publishers Inc., San Francisco (2011)
5. Hand, D.J., Smyth, P., Mannila, H.: Principles of Data Mining. MIT Press, Cambridge (2001)
6. Hoque, N., Ahmed, H., Bhattacharyya, D., Kalita, J.: A fuzzy mutual information-based feature selection method for classification. Fuzzy Inf. Eng. 8(3), 355–384 (2016)
7. Hoque, N., Singh, M., Bhattacharyya, D.K.: EFS-MI: an ensemble feature selection method for classification. Complex Intell. Syst. 4(2), 105–118 (2018)

8. Liang, S., Liu, Y., Wang, C., Jian, L.: Design and evaluation of a parallel K-nearest neighbor algorithm on CUDA-enabled GPU. In: 2010 IEEE 2nd Symposium on Web Society, pp. 53–60, August 2010. https://doi.org/10.1109/SWS.2010.5607480
9. Lippert, A.: NVIDIA GPU architecture for general purpose computing (2009). Accessed 10 June 2018
10. Sgandurra, D., Muñoz-González, L., Mohsen, R., Lupu, E.C.: Automated dynamic analysis of ransomware: benefits, limitations and use for detection. arXiv preprint arXiv:1609.03020 (2016)
11. Tan, P.N.: Introduction to Data Mining. Pearson Education India (2018)

Cluster-Based Regression Model for Predicting Aqueous Solubility of the Molecules

Priyanka Shit[✉] and Haider Banka

Indian Institute of Technology (ISM) Dhanbad, Dhanbad, Jharkhand, India
priyanka15.ism@gmail.com

Abstract. Prediction of physicochemical properties is a crucial step in the drug discovery process. It is a combination of various tasks; one of the essential steps in that process is aqueous solubility prediction. Aqueous solubility (logS) is a significant feature which is used to determine the drug-likeness of any compound. There are various machine learning, and statistical methods have been used to predict aqueous solubility in the literature. In this study, the aim is to propose a model which will improve the performance of the prediction model. In this study, data samples have clustered in different groups and built the regression model for each cluster. After that, the aqueous solubility value of each entity has predicted according to the cluster model. Combination of K-Means with various regression models has used for clustering and prediction purpose, respectively. Performance of the proposed model evaluated us- ing Root Mean square error statistical measure. We have compared all the regression models with cluster-based model and got the best result with a cluster-based random forest model, which has RMSE value 0.6 and 0.61 for dataset 1 and dataset 2 respectively.

Keywords: Aqueous solubility · Drug-likeness · Clustering · Regression

1   Introduction

Aqueous solubility prediction is one of the challenging tasks among the drug discovery process and other applications. It can be used to determine the drug-likeness of any compound and also important for prediction of ADMET (absorption, distribution, metabolism, excretion, and toxicity) properties [1, 2]. Human blood consists of 80% of water so, the compounds with low water solubility having low absorption rate. Therefore, prediction of aqueous solubility in an early phase of drug discovery and development process can help to re- duce the time and cost factors. It also eliminates the molecules, which have very low aqueous solubility for reducing the risk of failure. Most of these are QSAR (Quantitative-Structure-Activity Relationship) methods where the activity of any molecule generate by mapping and encoding the structure of that molecule. Structures encode by undirected graph representation and mapping to specific length feature vectors. Chemical compounds can also be represented using SMILES notations, which is a standard representation and used to extract other information about that compound from chemical databases [3]. It is imperative to find a suitable regression or classification

© Springer Nature Switzerland AG 2020
R. Patgiri et al. (Eds.): BigDML 2019, CCIS 1317, pp. 14–24, 2020.
https://doi.org/10.1007/978-3-030-62625-9_2

model to learn the input training samples. There are various computational models have been applied to solve chemoinformatics problems [4]. Literature reflects significant work in the area of multiple properties prediction. Literature reflects significant work in the area of properties prediction like Quantitative Structure-Property Relationships Models (QSPR) [5, 6], Use of Deep learning for a molecular graph representation of drug-like molecules [7], the role of solubility oral absorption prediction using a decision tree [8], Random forest model [9], theoretical models [10, 11], kinetic and intrinsic solubility prediction by potentiometric [12], multi-linear regression model, theoretical physics with machine learning models [13]. In this study, the aqueous solubility of molecules has predicted using six regression models. Here, the main aim to improve the performance of the predictive model. For this purpose, Data samples have clustered before applying to the predictive regression model. All molecules have represented in terms of molecular descriptors, which are the inputs for the predictive model. The descriptions of all methodologies are in Sect. 2. Aqueous solubility has predicted using the proposed model and also without clustering approach. Statistical performance measures have used to compare the simulation results of existing regression models with clustering approach.

2   Materials and Methods

2.1   Dataset

In this study, we have used two datasets; one of them is a small dataset of the only drug-like molecule, and another is a relatively large dataset with mixed data on drugs and non-drugs molecules. The details of each dataset have given in Table 1. We have collected SDF format, and molecular descriptors have extracted using the freely available PaDEL software.

Table 1. Dataset details

Dataset	Total samples	Training	Testing	Resource
Dataset 1	745	595	150	Ref [14]
Dataset 2	1708	1366	342	Ref [15]

2.2   Physicochemical Properties

All the molecules have collected in SDF format from the previous literature and manually from databases. Molecular descriptors can be estimated using various online server or using the software. In this study, we have used freely available PaDEL software for physicochemical properties calculation. Initially, we have taken 1185 features and after applying feature reduction methods the reduced feature set is 19. The reduced features, which have used for this study are XLogP, Hydrogen bond acceptor, Hydrogen bond donor, HybRatio, TopoPSA, AlogP, MlogP, Lipoaffinity index, Hydrogen atom count, Oxygen count, CrippenLogP, bpol, molecular weight, Mcgowan Volume, Kappa Indices, CrippenMR, FracC, Ring count, Rotatable bond count.

2.3 Feature Selection

Chemo-informatics deals with drug discovery process which involved a huge number of compounds with different types of chemical properties. So it is very important to reduce feature space to enhance the prediction performance Feature reduction provides faster and cost-effective predictive algorithms and it also helps to understand the underlying process that generated the data which is a very important step in machine learning process. In order to reduce the no of irrelevant features in this study, relief and Pearson correlation methods have used for feature selection.

Relief: Relief is a feature selection algorithm which uses a statistical method. It can handle both discrete and continuous type features. It runs in low order polynomial time and independent to heuristic search. It takes linear time and effective when the instances are large in number. It computes weights and ranking of all the features for any input data samples using the target vector. This is effective for classification and also for the regression problem. The feature weight value is ranging from -1 to $+1$ [16, 17].

Pearson Correlation: Pearson Correlation is a basic feature reduction technique which is used to measure the linear dependency or correlation between two features [18]. The outcome of this method lies in the range of -1 to $+1$, both values are inclusive. Where $+1$ is for the positive correlation, -1 is for negative correlation and 0 is no correlation. The correlation is calculated by the following equation:

$$\gamma = \frac{\sum XY - \frac{(\sum X)*(\sum Y)}{n}}{\sqrt{(\sum X^2 - \frac{(\sum X)^2}{n})*(\sum Y^2 - \frac{(\sum Y)^2}{n})}} \tag{1}$$

Where X and Y are the features between which correlation is Calculated and n is the number of samples.

2.4 Clustering

Cluster analysis or clustering approach is based on an unsupervised learning approach in which the grouping of data samples takes place according to their similarity. Data samples in each group are more similar to the data sample of the same group as compare to other groups. Clustering is most important to visualize the data effectively. There are various types of clustering algorithms like connectivity models, centroid models, distributive models, density models etc. according to their application in the literature, K-Means algorithm is one of the popular centroid models clustering techniques.

K-Means Clustering Algorithm: It is based on an iterative process where the main aim of each iteration is to find local maxima. K-Means algorithm [18, 19] can be described by following steps:

- Step 1: Specify a desirable number of clusters.
- Step 2: Assign data points randomly in each cluster.
- Step 3: Compute centroids of each cluster.

- Step 4: According to closest cluster centroid reassign each data points.
- Step 5: Recompute cluster centroids.
- Step 6: Repeat steps 4 and 5 or terminates if no improvement possible and reach global optima.

2.5 Regression Analysis

A regression analysis widely used statistical method in which relationship among the variables estimated. It is used for prediction or forecasting so it also comes under as machine learning approaches. It helps to understand that what the effect on the dependent variable is when values of the independent variable are changed. In this method, problem is to find a variable or set of variables which are significant predictors of the required criterion variable. It may depend on a single independent variable or combination of a set of independent variables. There are various types of the regression model in the literature but in this study, we have used Gaussian Progress Regression, Multi-Linear Regression, Neural Net Regression, Ensemble Regression, Random Forest Regression, SVM Regression predictive models for comparative study [20–23]. All the given regression models have been used with and without cluster-based model for comparative study.

2.6 Statistical Performance Measures

In this study, to compare the result and performance Analysis of prediction model we have used Root Mean Square Error (RMSE) as Statistical performance matrices:

$$RMSE = \sqrt{\frac{1}{n}\sum_{i=1}^{n}(Y_i^{Actual} - Y_i^{Predicted})^2} \tag{2}$$

3 Proposed Model

Aqueous solubility or other physiochemical properties have been predicted using various regression models in the previous studies. In this study, the main aim of the proposed model to increase the performance of the prediction model by clustering the data samples. The steps of the proposed model have been described in Fig. 1. So for this, in the first step, we have taken the solubility dataset which has been described in the previous section. All the data samples are represented in terms of molecular descriptors. Few molecular descriptors have been selected from the huge feature space for this study. For the selection of relevant features, there are various techniques like Filter, wrapper or subset selection. For this model, combination of relief and Pearson correlation method has been used as a feature selection method. Then data samples have been clustered according to their similarity. Clustering is important to visualize the data according to similarity and dissimilarity among them. Data samples which are more similar they belong to the same group or cluster. Regression analysis is a set of statistical processes

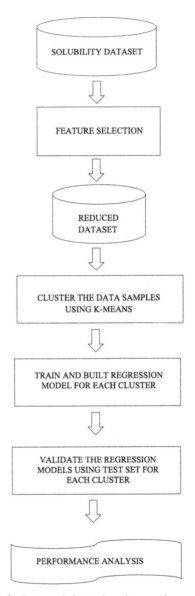

Fig. 1. Proposed cluster-based regression model

in which the value of the single variable is estimated in terms of other variables which is represented as the equation. Mapping all data in a single equation is very difficult for a large sample set. When the size of the data set is increased then mean absolute error is also increased. In regression analysis error is calculated in term of difference in actual and predicted value. So to reduce the error of predictive model data samples have been clustered before prediction in the proposed model. After clustering the data samples regression model is implemented for each cluster. The aqueous solubility of each new sample has been predicted after assigning to a specific cluster and the target value is calculated according to the cluster equation. This step reduces the overall mean absolute error which improves the performance of the predictive model. It eliminates the limitation of a single regression model. In this model, K-Means have been used as a clustering technique and for prediction, various regression models have been used like Gaussian regression, multi-linear, neural net regression, ensemble regression, random forest regression, SVM regression. Using K-Means clustering data has divided into more than one group. After clustering for each group we have trained the model and finding different regression equation. For validation, the predicted value is calculated for each equation and finds the average and compares the result with actual log S value. In the last step for performance analysis, root mean square error (RMSE) has used as statistical performance matrices and compare the performance of other given regression model with the proposed cluster-based regression predictive model. The outcomes of this model have been described in the next section.

4   Result and Discussion

Aqueous solubility dataset 1 and dataset 2 collected from the resources was in SDF form, so features have extracted for this using PaDEL software. There is a huge set of physiochemical properties to represent any compound, so it is also a challenging task to select the properties which give more accurate values of other property. In this study, for feature selection, we have used relief feature selection and after that Pearson Correlation i.e. a combination of both methods have used. Relief is an effective model which is used to select best-ranked features and Pearson correlation has been used to eliminate redundancy of the feature set and also used to select most relevant features which are highly correlated with the target. So the combination of both techniques performs better with given predictive models. For prediction purpose, we have used 6 different regression models and compared the performance of each model with and without a proposed cluster-based model. All predictive models have trained and tested using MATLAB and WEKA software. The training and testing phase results for each dataset has represented in tabular form Table 2, Table 3 respectively.

Table 2. Training and Test phase Phase results for Dataset 1 with and without a cluster-based model

Regression model	Without clustering		With clustering	
	Training RMSE	Testing RMSE	Training RMSE	Testing RMSE
Gaussian regression	0.70	0.81	0.65	0.75
Multi-linear regression	0.67	0.79	0.60	0.72
Neural net regression	0.66	0.80	0.60	0.78
Ensemble regression	0.65	0.81	0.65	0.80
Random forest	0.53	0.65	0.50	0.60
SVM regression	0.70	0.83	0.68	0.75

Table 3. Training and Test phase Phase result for Dataset 2 with and without a cluster-based model

Regression model	Without clustering		With clustering	
	Training RMSE	Testing RMSE	Training RMSE	Testing RMSE
Gaussian regression	0.77	0.79	0.63	0.65
Multi-linear regression	0.82	0.86	0.70	0.72
Neural net regression	0.84	0.88	0.53	0.79
Ensemble regression	0.55	0.77	0.45	0.66
Random forest	0.45	0.72	0.36	0.61
SVM regression	0.85	0.88	0.70	0.73

Table 2 is the result summary of dataset 1 training and test phase in which, we have got the best result with cluster-based random forest model. For dataset 1 best outcome RMSE, 0.60 is with using two cluster centers. Due to small data samples by increasing number of centers performance also decreases. Figure 2 and Fig. 3 is regression plot of training phase and test phase random forest model for dataset 1 respectively. Due to biased and small dataset of only drug-like molecules the result is not significantly improved using cluster based model.

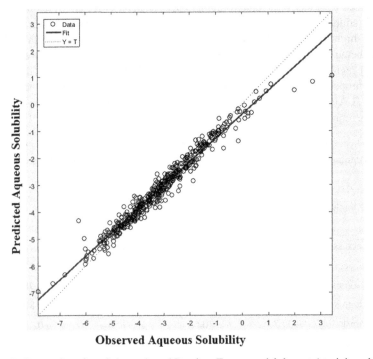

Fig. 2. Regression plot of cluster-based Random Forest model dataset 1 training phase

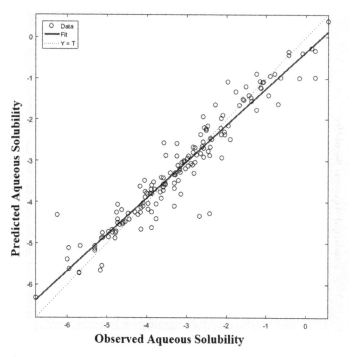

Fig. 3. Regression plot of cluster-based Random Forest model dataset 1 test phase

Therefore we have also taken another relatively large dataset of mixed molecules and compared the result. The original work has been done using dataset 2 and dataset 1 has taken only for comparative study for different sample size dataset. In Table 2, we can see that in the training phase error is less as compare to Table 3 but test result has not improved. Except random forest model using other model for dataset 1 performance is low. Due to small sample size if we increase the number of clusters predictive model is not perform effectively. For dataset 2 optimum number of clusters is 4, above this performance decreases relatively in this experiment. In Table 3, training phase error is very low for random forest model in both cases and also gives best result with this model. Figure 4 and Fig. 5 are the representation of regression plots for training and test phase of best model using actual and predicted solubility values.

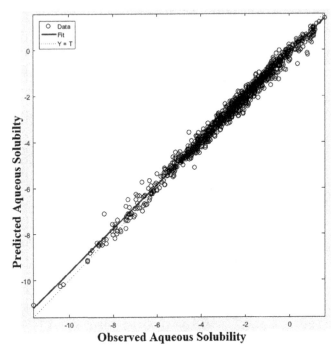

Fig. 4. Regression plot of cluster-based Random Forest model dataset 2 training phase

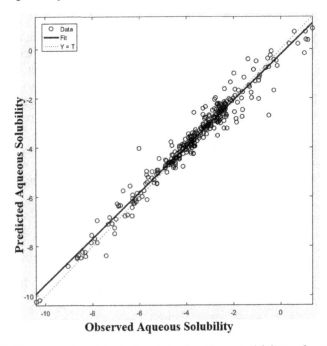

Fig. 5. Regression plot of cluster-based Random Forest model dataset 2 test phase

5 Conclusion

Predicting aqueous solubility is a critical task in the area of chemo-informatics. In this study, we have used two types of dataset one is a minimal sample size, and another is a relatively large sample. In both cases, with clustering or without clustering, we got the best result with a random forest regression model. We have got the lowest RMSE of 0.60 and 0.61 for dataset 1 and dataset 2 test phase respectively. For getting more improved unbiased results, a vast dataset should use. In this cluster-based model, we have got a good result with only using two clusters and four clusters for dataset 1 and dataset 2 respectively. For other datasets, the number of groups may vary.

References

1. Wang, J., Hou, T.: Recent advances on aqueous solubility prediction. Comb. Chem. High Throughput Screen. **14**(5), 328–338 (2011)
2. Murdande, S.B., et al.: Aqueous solubility of crystalline and amorphous drugs: challenges in measurement. Pharm. Dev. Technol. **16**(3), 187–200 (2011)
3. O'Boyle, N.M., et al.: Open babel: an open chemical toolbox. J. Cheminform. **3**(1), 33 (2011)
4. Habibi, N., et al.: A review of machine learning methods to predict the solubility of overexpressed recombinant proteins in Escherichia coli. BMC Bioinform. **15**(1), 134 (2014)
5. Hongmao, S.: A Practical Guide to Rational Drug Design. Woodhead Publishing, Cambridge (2015)
6. Schroeter, T.S., et al.: Estimating the domain of applicability for machine learning QSAR models: a study on aqueous solubility of drug discovery molecules. J. Comput.-Aided Mol. Des. **21**(9), 485–498 (2007)
7. Lusci, A., Pollastri, G., Baldi, P.: Deep architectures and deep learning in chemoinformatics: the prediction of aqueous solubility for drug-like molecules. J. Chem. Inf. Model. **53**(7), 1563–1575 (2013)
8. Newby, D., Freitas, A.A., Ghafourian, T.: Decision trees to characterise the roles of permeability and solubility on the prediction of oral absorption. Eur. J. Med. Chem. **90**, 751–765 (2015)
9. Palmer, D.S., et al.: Random forest models to predict aqueous solubility. J. Chem. Inf. Model. **47**(1), 150–158 (2007)
10. Palmer, D.S., et al.: First-principles calculation of the intrinsic aqueous solubility of crystalline druglike molecules. J. Chem. Theory Comput. **8**(9), 3322–3337 (2012)
11. Palmer, D.S., et al.: Predicting intrinsic aqueous solubility by a thermodynamic cycle. Mol. Pharm. **5**(2), 266–279 (2008)
12. Narasimham, L., Barhate, V.D.: Kinetic and intrinsic solubility determination of some β-blockers and antidiabetics by potentiometry. J. Pharm. Res. **4**(2), 532–536 (2011)
13. McDonagh, J.L., Nath. N., De Ferrari, L., Van Mourik, T., Mitchell, J.B.O: Uniting cheminformatics and chemical theory to predict the intrinsic aqueous solubility of crystalline druglike molecules. J. Chem. Inf. Model. **54**(3), 844–856 (2014)
14. Kumar, R., et al.: Classification of oral bioavailability of drugs by machine learning approaches: a comparative study. J. Comp. Interdisc. Sci. **2**(9), 1–18 (2011)
15. Hou, T.J., et al.: ADME evaluation in drug discovery. 4. Prediction of aqueous solubility based on atom contribution approach. J. Chem. Inf. Comput. Sci. **44**(1), 266–275 (2004)
16. Wang, J., et al.: Development of reliable aqueous solubility models and their application in druglike analysis. J. Chem. Inf. Model. **47**(4), 1395–1404 (2007)

17. Urbanowicz, R.J., et al.: Benchmarking relief-based feature selection methods. arXiv preprint arXiv:1711.08477 (2017)
18. Chandrashekar, G., Sahin, F.: A survey on feature selection methods. Comput. Electr. Eng. **40**(1), 16–28 (2014)
19. Stanforth, R.W.: Extending K-means clustering for analysis of quantitative structure activity relationships (QSAR). Diss. University of London (2008)
20. Smits, G.F., Jordaan, E.M.: Improved SVM regression using mixtures of kernels. In: Proceedings of the 2002 International Joint Conference on Neural Networks, 2002, IJCNN 2002, vol. 3. IEEE (2002)
21. Kaytez, F., et al.: Forecasting electricity consumption: a comparison of regression analysis, neural networks and least squares support vector machines. Int. J. Electr. Power Energy Syst. **67**, 431–438 (2015)
22. Svetnik, V., et al.: Random forest: a classification and regression tool for compound classification and QSAR modeling. J. Chem. Inf. Comput. Sci. **43**(6), 1947–1958 (2003)
23. Montgomery, D.C., Peck, E.A., Vining, G.G.: Introduction to Linear Regression Analysis, vol. 821. Wiley, Hoboken (2012)

A Preventive Intrusion Detection Architecture Using Adaptive Blockchain Method

Pratima Sharma[1(✉)], Rajni Jindal[1], and Malaya Dutta Borah[2]

[1] Delhi Technological University, Delhi, India
pratima.sharma1491@gmail.com, rajnijindal@dce.ac.in
[2] National Institute of Technology Silchar, Silchar, India
malayaduttaborah@cse.nits.ac.in

Abstract. This paper presents a network intrusion behavior detection utilizing an adaptive blockchain mechanism. A Layered Voting Rule System (LVRS) is introduced, which contains a positive layer, negative layer and propagation layer which trains the blockchain using the power consumption of the users to transfer and receive the data. The performance of the network is analyzed using Quality of Service (QoS) parameters, including throughput and power consumption. The observed throughput and power consumption of the proposed model is improved by more than 30% as compared to the model without blockchain.

Keywords: Layered Voting Rule System · Blockchain · Intrusion · Adaptive behavior

1 Introduction

The virtual world was built as the true global infrastructure when our technology system introduces both computer technology and network technology. The virtual world today is nearly as powerful as the real economy, placed as the basis for the corporate system. However, at the time when the information, in particular, the business information, exchanges online, a trustworthy authority is essential and necessary to ensure the credibility of the data and the actual value that can be grouped into the real world. This type of mode is the internet's company mode now. These so-called trusted parties, however, may also be likely and able to do some malicious and harmful things knowingly or unknowingly, such as tracking or selling customer data for company use [1].

Blockchain is suggested as a prospective alternative to the above issue. Blockchain is relatively an advanced technology that allows multiple authoritative domains which do not trust each other to collaborate, cooperate, and coordinate in a decision-making process. The advent of blockchain provides credible information management and exchange methods that can make internet transactions more real and free of third parties [2]. Various blockchain-based applications used to deliver company and other services that have a major effect on the online business system. Blockchain provides online transfer of data with non-modifiable data records, making the transfer of data more reliable. The blockchain boom is an integral part of the network, especially for the online business.

© Springer Nature Switzerland AG 2020
R. Patgiri et al. (Eds.): BigDML 2019, CCIS 1317, pp. 25–35, 2020.
https://doi.org/10.1007/978-3-030-62625-9_3

Blockchain-based applications can help to create internet reality and achieve fairness, equality, and sharing between online virtual reality in the real world. The object produced by blockchain technology in the non-real globe for the confirmed data becomes valuable and authentic. Blockchain will also play a more critical role in the future if online privacy and reliability become increasingly essential. Blockchain-based systems will be the basic infrastructure that can provide people with a wealth of services [3]. Chain management is applied when there is a need for a data transfer policy to maximize the efficiency of resource sharing. When one node in the network starts the data transfer to another node in the system, it is often observed that the source node includes other nodes in the transaction to a form a route. The intermediate nodes are referred to as hop in any chain architecture. As shown in Fig. 1, the source node aims to transfer the data to the destination node. To maximize resource utilization, one node becomes a data vendor for multiple nodes. This increases the randomness in the network, and the network becomes vulnerable to the intruders.

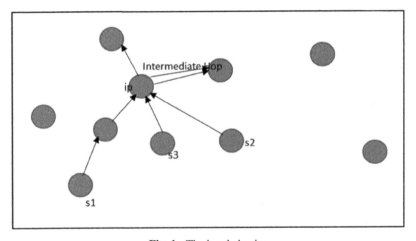

Fig. 1. The hop behavior

As shown in Fig. 1, if the intermediate node represented by "ip" receives a lot of data packets or data elements from source nodes s1, s2, s3 ... sn and so on, the intruder may also attempt to transfer the data from "ip" which will further affect the network environment. If described practically, every network has a network admin, but the network admin does not aim to identify the intruder, it would instead go to find the node in its system, which is intruded. As a user is using AVG antivirus. The antivirus cannot do anything to the virus generator, but it prevents its network from the effects of the virus. This paper focuses on this logic and prepares a Layered Voting Rule System (LVRS) whose description is given in Sect. 3.

The rest of the paper is organized as follows. Section 2 explains the related work. Section 3 provides detailed information on the proposed architecture. In Sect. 4, the assessment of the results is presented. The paper is concluded in Sect. 5.

2 Related Work

Meng et al. (2018) presented a study of the integration of Intrusion Detection System (IDS) and Blockchain Technology. The context of this type of intrusion detection and blockchain addresses its application in its route to migrate the issues of information exchange and trust calculation cooperatively. Blockchain technology is an emerging possibility for decentralized activities and information management without a trusted third party. Khan et al. (2018) presented a survey of primary security issues related to the Internet of Things (IoT). It categorized the most critical security issues and its regard to the IoT layered structure and, different protocols used in networking also been discussed. This work shows the difference between current work and past work related to the IoT, even the security issue against the existing IoT security problem. The suggested work also defines open research issues and IoT safety difficulties. Banerjee et al. (2018) with the assistance of several observations, the IoT safety option suggested by authors, included the absence of public access in the IoT dataset used by the researcher and practitioner. They also included the possibly delicate elements of the IoT dataset; after this, they discuss the capacity of blockchain technologies in enabling safe storage of IT dataset, there is a need to create a normal stakeholder for this processing. Li et al. (2018) presented the background and recent situation of the intrusion detection system, the characteristics and its ranking in the specific situation. It is a kind of technology which protects the network security from the attacks. It is also useful in detecting the speed and improving the integrity of the data security infrastructure. In this, they applied the technology to the blockchain information security model. Kim et al. (2018) presented three types of intrusion detection model for the bitcoin exchange and gave the detection and mitigation system with the help of the blockchain analysis. The main justification for the monitoring and mitigation system exploits the decentralized and governmental behavior of bitcoin blockchain as a fail-safe way to complete the present time system. Advanced technology offers the ability to search for intrusion in real time, which cannot be provided by current job. Kolekar et al. (2018) proposed state-of-the-art, hidden wall strings. In four dimensions, we assess both in-generation and study schemes: disseminated ledger, intrusion detection, blockchain project, consensus protocol, and insightful agreement. They also conclude that the current BLOCKBENCH, skeleton criteria for understanding the effectiveness of private blockchain and government blockchain. Blockchain methods have been a substantial secure power in recent years. Blockchains are shared ledgers that allow sides that do not support each other continuously to maintain several ecumenical nations. The parties agree on states' easiness, norms, and background. Li. et al. (2019) presented a CBSigIDS which is a design of Cooperative Block-chained Signature-based IDSs. It is used to create and renew a reliable tag database in an IoT setting. CBSigIDS provide a solution for integrated architectures without the need for a reliable intermediary. The results show that the calculation of CBSigIDS can improve the toughness and performance of signature-based IDSs in adversarial cases. Collaborative Intrusion Detection Network (CIDN) has become an important and essential security option for safeguarding IoT systems, enabling distinct IDS nodes to swap information with each other, e.g., regulations. However, evil nodes in a CIDN can generate untruthful tags and communicate with others, which can considerably degrade tracking effectiveness and robustness. Signorini et al. (2018) proposed a method called ADvISE: the first anomaly detection tool for a blockchain system which gives blockchain metadata, named forks, for the addition of collect potential malicious request in the present network system to escape the attacks. ADvISE add-on and analyzes the malicious forks for the creation of a threat database that provide the detection and prevention of future attacks. In general, ADvISE give permission to the detection of the abnormal transaction and protect them for being further spread.

3 Proposed Architecture

The proposed architecture monitors the entire data stream as the primary input to the monitoring system, and the users are connected to form the blockchain. The proposed work adopts a behavioral framework. The proposed architecture is named as LVRS, which contains three layers, a positive layer, a negative layer, and a propagation layer, as shown in Fig. 2.

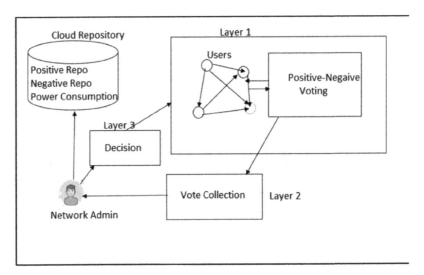

Fig. 2. Proposed architecture

Layer 1: The nodes are deployed in the network, and the nodes also referred to as users start sharing the resources from one end to another end. Blockchain technology is utilized for deploying the user nodes. Each user node stores the information in the form of ledger. Further, ledger information is utilized by the network admin for identifying the intruder node. The voting rule is based on the users, and each user had an independent set of data. The user design creates a semi-autonomous blockchain mechanism as each user is partially affected by another user who votes for him or against him. The sustainability of the user is dependent upon the positive votes, which is further controlled by the network administrator. The demanding user is referred to as destination, and the original resource holder is designated as the source in the proposed work. Each data transfer will also involve intermediate nodes, which are referred to as hop in the proposed work. Each data transfer is counted as one vote from source to destination vice and versa. The intermediate nodes are also benefited if the data is transferred successfully.

Layer 2: Layer 2 is operated by the Network Admin. The voting points are stored with the Network Admin at the Cloud Layer. Positive Layer Repository (PLR) and Negative Layer Repository (NLR) is created from the voting of the source to destination. Also, the power consumption in each simulative iteration of individual nodes and the total transfer is stored.

Layer 3: The third layer propagates the power consumption in combination with the positive repository and the negative repository. This layer decides whether the user is safe for resource sharing or not. LVRS further bifurcates the propagation layer identification mechanism in subsequent steps in which the first step is for the propagation mechanism, and the second step uses gradient functions, which is followed by linear quad architecture for data propagation. LVRS analyses the behavior of the user based on the propagation data, which is generated through the overall power consumption in transactions. A unique voting rule is presented in the paper, which helps in analyzing the network when it is scanned for the intrusion.

The workflow of the proposed architecture is described as follows:

a) The users are deployed with random locations in the network.
b) The users will share the data as a resource sharing mechanism.
c) The input data, i.e., the data user wants to transfer or share from one end to another end, can be sent only once in one simulation.
d) One data transfer will be considered as one vote to the destination.
e) Source and destinations are assumed to be immune from intrusion as the network considers the vote as a positive effect to the immunity.
f) The Network Admin (NA) has a veto power to reject the vote count of any node if NA feels like the node is compromised.
g) NA uses the blockchain mechanism in three layers of processing and stores the information in the cloud.

It is assumed that every intruded node which is involved in the data transfer, will consume more power but every high energy consuming node cannot be considered as intruded. The overall proposed structure is demonstrated in Fig. 3(a), Fig. 3(b) and Fig. 3(c) as follows.

As shown in Fig. 3(a), when a source 's' transfer the data to 'd' successfully, the network admin counts it as a positive vote whereas, Fig. 3(b) shows that if the node is not able to transfer the data to 'd' successfully, the node suffers a penalty. It is assumed that 65% of the total transmitted data is received at the destination end, the transaction is said to be successful transaction and the network admin stores the information of the source node and the hops in blocks to rate the node between 0.50 to 1.0. The rating is done based on the total amount of actual data transfer from one end to another. If the node is involved in any other transaction, the average weight of all the previous operations and the current transaction is considered. If the transaction is not successful, i.e., if the

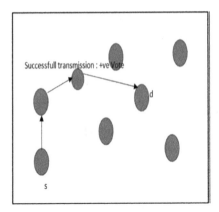

Fig. 3(a). Positive vote

received amount is less than 65%, the source node gets a penalty between 0.1 to 0.49, and hence. The negative weight is updated. The hops in the network also get penalty between 0.1 to 0.20. At the time of the network scan, if the node has a weight more than 0.60, the node is free from the scan. A node having a negative rating more than 0.20 is scanned twice at the time of the scan. The nodes are also referred to as users in our proposed model.

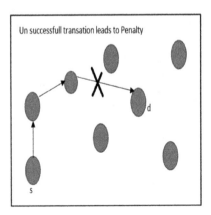

Fig. 3(b). Penalty

Figure 3(c) represents the decision-making architecture of LVRS, which involves Positive Layer Repo (PLR) and Negative Layer Repo (NLR) as discussed earlier. In addition to the PLR and NLR network, admin also keeps a record of consumed power in the data transaction through each user in the network and uses it for decision making to find any intrusion in the network. The nomenclature of all used variables is given in Table 2. The description of identification is as follows. The users are deployed randomly in the network with a random position. The ordinal measures of deployment are illustrated in Table 1.

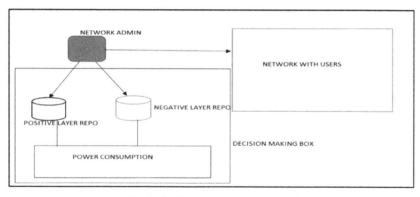

Fig. 3 (c). Decision making of LVRS

Table 1. Deployment parameters

Total user count	40–60
Deployment mode	Random
Data type	Bits
Area of deployment	1000 × 1000 m
Selection mode	Random
Total number of simulations	100–1000
Deployment tool	Anaconda
Deployment framework	Spyder
Language used	Python

Table 2. Nomenclature of variables

Variable	Description
P_t	Amount of power required to transfer a data packet
P_r	Amount of power consumption for receiving a data packet
$Consumed_{Power}$	Total power consumed by the node
$Model_{Weight}$	Weight given by the model to a node
$Input_{Architeture}$	Initial power consumption
$window_{size}$	Window size

The proposed model considers a power consumption model when it comes to transferring the data from one end to another. When a user must transfer the data from one end to another, it will consume P_t amount of power. Similarly, P_r is the power consumption to receive the data element. NA keeps a record of transfer and receiving of the data elements along with the users who are involved in the data transfer. P_t and P_r is heterogeneous, i.e., it is different for every node. A maximum of 1000 simulations is monitored with a breakpoint after every 100 simulations; hence, the window size of identification is 100. The NA analyses the network after every 100 simulations and can use his veto power at any instance. NA uses power consumption as the main identifying attribute. P_r and P_t has two sub-attributes. The user will consume less power under normal condition and more power under intruded conditions. The pseudo code of node deployment and data transfer with voting is as follows.

Pseudo Code of Node Deployment:

1. Input: $User_{Count}$
2. For_{each} user in $user_{count}$
3. $User_x =$ Deployment_Mode.Random()
4. $User_y =$ Deployment_Mode.Random()
5. Generate $Power_{ConsumptionModel}$
6. Destination = Generate a random destination.
7. Source = Look for the resources from the destination
8. $Intermediate_{Hops} =$ Generate Resource Carrier
9. Initialize Network
10. Start Stimulation and Data Transfer

The pseudo code deploys the user with random x and y axis in the network. Every user contains some resource which is sharable in the network. A power consumption model is also deployed, which clarifies the total consumption of power when the user receives a data packet and total consumed power when a node receives a data packet. The data is transferred through intermediate hops which have any vacant slot to transfer the data. The data are documents which are available with the user. The resources are not editable; only the owner of the data has the authority to edit the data of the document. The rest of the users have read-only permission.

Identification of Power Consumption
$For_{each} establi$ shedconnection between User1 to User 2

$$Consumed_{Power} = \sum_{k=0}^{n} P_t + P_r \tag{1}$$

$$Prevention_{Input_{Architecture}} = Consumed\_Power \tag{2}$$

Initialize Chain Mechanism with $Prevention_{Input_{Architecture}}$
Propagate Chain with linear and Quad propagation model.

$$Linear\ Model\ follows : ax + b = 0 \tag{3}$$

$$Quad\ Model\ follows : ax^2 + bx + c = 0 \tag{4}$$

$$Chain_{Weight} = Model_{Weight} + Input_{Architeture} \tag{5}$$

$$Chain_{SatisfyingElement} = Average_{Gradient} + window_{size} \tag{6}$$

$$Average_{Gradient} = \sum_{i}^{window_{size}} Consumed_{Power}$$

If the gradient is satisfied, then cross-validated using block-chain. Cross-validation is done using the same model, which is done to satisfy the chain training. After 1000 simulations, the result of every window is analyzed, and the max affected user is barred, and his/her voting is discarded, and the user is barred in the network.

4 Results

The results are evaluated using the following parameters.

a) Throughput: Total received packets per time frame.
b) Power Consumption: Total consumed power in each window/after total simulation.

Every result is evaluated with the window defined in Sect. 3. Figure 4 represents the throughput of the proposed model with a comparison of the model without blockchain. The throughput of the proposed architecture is high as compared to the network model with no intrusion model. The proposed algorithm has adopted the new intrusion model, which is adaptive and hence, the chances of network intrusion is quite low. The throughput is tested for a maximum of 500 simulation iterations. The average throughput for proposed architecture is noticed to be 13000 whereas, for the generalized network architecture, it stands 8700. A noticeable difference of $(13000–8700)/1300 = 33\%$ is noticed.

The proposed architecture is also evaluated for power consumption, as shown in Fig. 5. A Total of 500 simulations is tested based on Power Consumption. A noticeable difference in power consumption is observed. The power consumption of the proposed architecture is low as compared to the network model with no intrusion model.

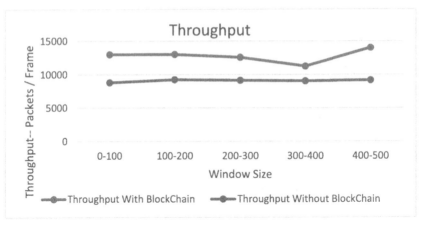

Fig. 4. Throughput

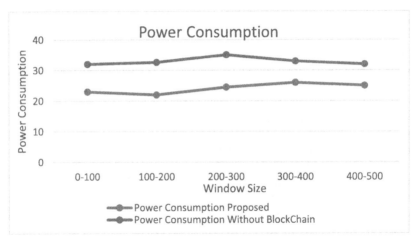

Fig. 5. Power consumption

5 Conclusion

This paper presented an intrusion behavior analysis architecture through adaptive blockchain behavior of intruders. Power consumption is kept as the critical aspect of the intrusion analysis. The proposed architecture is named as LVRS, which contains different layers for a different purpose. A positive layer, a negative layer, and a propagation layer are presented in the paper which utilizes power consumption. LVRS further bifurcates the identification mechanism in subsequent steps in which the first step is for the propagation mechanism, and the second step uses gradient functions, which is followed by linear quad architecture for data propagation. LVRS analyses the behavior of the user based on the propagation data, which is generated through the overall power consumption in transactions. A unique voting rule is presented in the paper, which helps in analyzing the network when it is scanned for the intrusion. A window size of 100 simulations is used to apply breakpoints and to analyze the data through breakpoints. A total of 500 simulations are tested based on Throughput and Power Consumption. A noticeable difference of more than 30% is observed in both throughput and power consumption.

References

Meng, W., Tischhauser, E.W., Wang, Q., Wang, Y., Han, J.: When intrusion detection meets blockchain technology: a review. IEEE Access **6**, 10179–10188 (2018)

Khan, M.A., Salah, K.: IoT security: review, blockchain solutions, and open challenges. Future Gener. Comput. Syst. **82**, 395–411 (2018)

Banerjee, M., Lee, J., Choo, K.K.R.: A blockchain future for the internet of things security: a position paper. Digit. Commun. Netw. **4**(3), 149–160 (2018)

Li, D., Cai, Z., Deng, L., Yao, X., Wang, H.H.: The information security model of blockchain based on intrusion sensing in the IoT environment. Cluster Comput. **22**, 451–468 (2018)

Kim, S., Kim, B., Kim, H.J.: Intrusion detection and mitigation system using blockchain analysis for bitcoin exchange. In: International Conference on Cloud Computing and Internet of Things, CCIOT 2018, pp. 40–44. Association for Computing Machinery, October, 2018

Kolekar, S.M., More, R.P., Bachal, S.S., Yenkikar, A.V.: Review paper on untwist blockchain: a data handling process of blockchain systems. In: International Conference on Information, Communication, Engineering, and Technology (ICICET), pp. 1–4. IEEE, August 2018

Li, W., Tug, S., Meng, W., Wang, Y.: Designing collaborative block chained signature-based intrusion detection in IoT environments. Future Gener. Comput. Syst. **96**, 481–489 (2019)

Signorini, M., Pontecorvi, M., Kanoun, W., Di Pietro, R.: Advise anomaly detection tool for blockchain systems. In: IEEE World Congress on Services (SERVICES), pp. 65–66. IEEE, July 2018

Automatic Extraction of Locations from News Articles Using Domain Knowledge

Loitongbam Sanayai Meetei$^{(\boxtimes)}$ ⓘ, Ringki Das, Thoudam Doren Singh ⓘ,
and Sivaji Bandyopadhyay

Department of Computer Science and Engineering, National Institute of Technology Silchar,
Silchar, Assam, India
loisanayai@gmail.com, ringkidas@gmail.com,
thoudam.doren@gmail.com, sivaji.cse.ju@gmail.com

Abstract. With the increasing amount of digital data, it is becoming increasingly hard to extract useful information from text data, especially for resource-constrained languages. In this work, we report the task of language-independent automatic extraction of locations from news articles using domain knowledge. The work is tested on four languages namely, English and three resource-constrained languages: Assamese, Manipuri and Mizo, the lingua francas of three neighboring North-Eastern states of India namely Assam, Manipur, and Mizoram respectively. Our architecture is based on semantic similarity between similar words based on the popular word embedding, word2vec model coupled with the domain knowledge of the aforementioned regions. The model is able to detect the best possible detailed locations.

Keywords: Location extraction · Word2vec · Word similarity · Resource constrained language · Assamese · Manipuri · Mizo

1 Introduction

The North-Eastern part of India (officially North Eastern Region) comprises of seven sister states with around 220 spoken languages. Assamese, Manipuri and Mizo, the lingua francas of three neighboring states: Assam, Manipur, and Mizoram respectively, belong to different language families. Assamese is the major language spoken in the North-Eastern part of India and an official language of Assam. It belongs to the Indo-European family of languages. Manipuri comes under the Tibeto-Burman language while Mizo is a Kuki-Chin language. Both Tibeto-Burman and Kuki-Chin are the subfamily of the Sino Tibetan language. Assamese is spoken by over 15 million speakers mainly in the Brahmaputra valley. The speaker of Manipuri and Mizo are around 3 million and 1 million respectively. The usage of all the three languages can be found in the Northeastern states as well as in the neighboring countries like Bangladesh and Myanmar. There are six major types of word order made up of three building blocks, namely Subject(S), Object(O) and Verb(V), namely: i) SVO, ii) SOV, iii) VSO iv) OSV v) VOS and vi) OVS. The word order of Assamese, English, Manipuri, and Mizo are SOV, SVO, SOV,

© Springer Nature Switzerland AG 2020
R. Patgiri et al. (Eds.): BigDML 2019, CCIS 1317, pp. 36–47, 2020.
https://doi.org/10.1007/978-3-030-62625-9_4

and OSV respectively. Even if Assamese and Manipuri belong to a different language family group, both the languages follow the SOV pattern. In some cases, the word order in the Assamese tends to be relatively free. Each of the three states is divided into 33, 9^1 and 8 districts in Assam, Manipur, and Mizoram respectively.

Named Entity Recognition (NER) is one of the popular tasks in natural language processing (NLP). The idea here is to identify and extract the named entities such as the names of persons, locations, organizations, etc. from a text. The state of the art of the NER system for a widely used language such as Chinese, English, etc. are close to the human brain. A quality NER system requires an annotated training corpus, however, for low resource-constrained languages, preparing such training corpus is a laborious task. Language-specific tools such as POS tagger which helps in enhancing the performance of the NER system is also not available for such languages.

In this paper, we proposed a language-independent system for the automatic extraction of locations from local daily news articles using domain knowledge. Here, the domain knowledge refers to a list of pre-defined names of the location in a region. Our system doesn't use language tools such as Part of Speech (POS) tagger and is based on word embedding and word similarity measure. Also, the system is able to identify the locations at the possible detailed location, such as at the locality level. The system can be used in a news recommendation system, disaster management, etc.

The rest of this paper is divided into four sections, with Sect. 2 discussing the related previous works. Section 3 and Sect. 4 describe the architecture used in the model and the analysis of experimental results respectively. Finally, summing up with the conclusion and future work in Sect. 5.

2 Literature Review

In the last decennium, word association has been well studied in linguistics. "Word Association" as a psycholinguistic term proposed by Church et al. [3] e.g. co-occurrence with other words, has a variety of applications which can be used in optical character recognition (OCR), speech recognition, information retrieval and enhancing the productivity of lexicographers.

Previous research works have carried out the study on the semantic similarity of text on different levels, such as word, sentence, and phrase, etc. The proposed model by Mihalcea et al. [9] was to find out the semantic similarity of short texts using Corpus and Knowledge-based. Along with the vector-based similarity approach, Microsoft paraphrase parallel corpus was used for the identification of paraphrase as well as to generate paraphrase. Islam et al. [6] proposed a semantic text similarity model (STS) for measuring similar text from semantic and syntactic information based on similar functions. A ranked-based system was generated by Wen et al. [16] for identifying synonyms which are based on the distributional hypothesis. Sentence similarity can be applied in many areas such as text mining, question-answering, and text summarizing according to Achananuparp et al. [1]. Wang et al. [15] developed a model to estimate sentence similarity with the help of the decomposition-composition vector and CNN (Convolution Neural Network) model.

---

[1] 16 districts as of December 2016, demarcation yet to be ascertained.

From a large dataset, two atypic models were suggested by Mikolov et al. [10] for computing continuous vector representation of words. It was remarked that at lower cost learning high-quality word vectors is better than neural networks. Skip-gram and CBOW (Continuous Bag of Words) can give better results than Neural Network Language Model and Recurrent Neural Network Language Model. A negative sampling is reported by Goldberg et al. [4] as an efficient approach to word embedding for finding out words having a similar meaning with similar context. It brings a different objective to the Skip-gram model.

The extraction of geolocation from text data was put forward for consideration by Imani et al. [5]. Named Entity Recognition tool has been used to identify geolocation from news articles using supervised classification and sentence embedding techniques at the country level. With the help of Named Entity Recognizer and geo-tagged tweets, the disaster location from Microblogs was extracted in Lingad et al. [7]. The affected area could be located as geographic locations like country, city, village, and river, etc. and point-of-interest could be hotels, shopping centers, and restaurants. Different tools such as Twitter, Open NLP, Standford NER, Yahoo! Place Maker for recognizing references to the location were used.

Named Entity Recognition (NER) is considered to be a baby step in the direction of Information Extraction which also plays a very vital role in Natural Language Processing (NLP). Existing works on NER for regional languages were carried out by [2, 12, 14]. Named Entity Recognition for the Assamese language was reported by Sharma et al. [12] using ruled based and supervised machine learning techniques such as Hidden Markov Models (HMM), Conditional Random Fields (CRF), Support Vector Machines (SVM) and Maximum Entropy (ME). Because of the scarcity of resources in a regional language, it is a very challenging task for their experiments. Recognition of named entity in Manipuri is reported by Singh et al. [14]. The authors developed two different models using an active learning technique and Support Vector Machine. A large amount of annotated corpora was used in both the models to recognize the location, person and organization names, designations, etc. For Mizo language a NER system is expressed by Bentham et al. [2] using a rule-based approach on news corpus. A Named Entity Extraction system was proposed by Nadeau et al. [11] using unsupervised techniques. To identify and classify entities from a given document the authors have to combine the Named Entity Extraction with Named Entity Disambiguation. The authors created a large cluster of semantically related words using seed words.

3   Architecture

A high-level graphical representation of the proposed schema is introduced in Fig. 1. The first step is a collection of data from different local daily newspapers in four different languages, namely Assamese, English, Manipuri, and Mizo. The data collection step is followed by the data cleaning process. Using the processed data, a word embedding model is trained using the word2vec. Finally, retrieving the candidate keywords based on the ranking of the cosine similarity distance with the seed words prepared with the help of domain knowledge. The approach of our model is described in the following sub-sections.

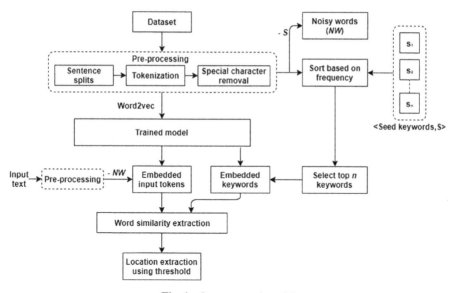

Fig. 1. Our proposed model

3.1 Data Collection

We prepared our dataset by collecting the news article from the local daily newspapers separately for Assamese[2], Manipuri[3] and Mizo[4] languages. Apart from this dataset, we also collected the news articles from the local daily newspaper of Manipur[5] reported in the English language. For Assamese and English languages, separate scrappers built inhouse using Java and its Jsoup library[6] is used. As for the Manipuri and Mizo language, we have used the dataset in [13] and [8] respectively. The news articles on the Assamese language are collected for the period of June 2018 to June 2019. While for English, Manipuri and Mizo[7] are collected for the period of July 2011 to May 2019, May 2008 to May 2010 and April 2013 to June 2019 respectively. The collected dataset is used as a training dataset for our model.

3.2 Pre-processing

Data collected from the news articles are in an unstructured format and contains several noisy texts. To process the data into a consumable format, the whole corpus grouped by language is subjected to a series of pre-processing steps separately.

The pre-processing step includes:

---

[2] https://www.asomiyapratidin.in/.

[3] https://www.thesangaiexpress.com/.

[4] https://www.vanglaini.org/.

[5] https://www.ifp.co.in/.

[6] https://jsoup.org/.

[7] We collected more dataset on [8].

1. Splitting the text into sentences.
2. Tokenization of a sentence into token of words.
3. Removing special characters and punctuation.
4. Replacing multiple spaces into a single space.
5. Removal of single-character tokens.
6. Normalize to lower case [only for Roman characters].

The result is a list of sentences for each of the languages. The details of the training corpus (number of sentences, number of tokens and the average number of tokens per sentence for each language) after the completion of the pre-processing are shown in Table 1. What can be clearly seen in Table 1 is that the dataset for Mizo language is the largest, followed by English, Manipuri and Assamese.

Table 1. Statistics of our training corpus of each of the languages.

Language	Sentences	Tokens	Avg tokens per sentence
Assamese	69416	839062	12
English	660444	17732538	26
Manipuri	104625	1988554	19
Mizo	746609	22431244	30

3.3 Word2vec

Word embedding is a vector representation of the text vocabulary, capable of highlighting the semantic or syntactic similarities or relations between words. One of the most popular technique to learn word embedding is word2vec, a shallow neural network model. The word2vec model consists of three main layers namely, an input layer, a hidden layer, and an output layer as shown in Fig. 2. The input layer is a text corpus with C context words where each word is represented by the one-hot encoding vector. The hidden layer is a fully-connected layer with n neurons whose weights are the word embedding. The output layer is a feature vector of length V. It groups the similar word vector into one vector space. The word2vec can be trained with either of the two language models: CBOW or Skip-gram. For building the word embedding, we used Gensim[8] which is a Python library for extracting document with similar semantic.

3.4 Feature Selection

The feature selection of our model consists of two main parts, namely, filtering of keywords and preparing a list of noisy words. Our main feature is the use of custom seed keywords after filtering based on domain knowledge of each region, namely Assam

---

[8] https://radimrehurek.com/gensim/.

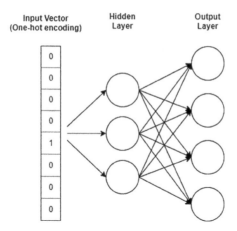

Fig. 2. Word2vec model

(news report in Assamese), Manipur (news report in English and Manipuri) and Mizoram (news report in Mizo). The following steps are applied dataset to a training to generate the final seed keywords:

1. Prepare list of keywords $(D = d_1, d_2 \ldots d_p)$ with names of popular locations of a region.
2. For each unique tokens $(T = t_1, t_2 \ldots t_n)$ in the training dataset, prepared their corresponding frequency list $(F = f_1, f_2 \ldots f_n)$ in the dataset.
3. Rank the keywords (D) based on their number of occurrences.
4. Select the top m highest frequency keywords, which is our final seed keywords $(K = k_1, k_2 \ldots k_m)$. The value of m range from 5 to 10.

Further, a list of top N highest frequency tokens are selected from F. However, we exclude any tokens present in D from the list. The value of N range from 100 to 150. Using these high-frequency words, we build a list of "noisy-words" (NW) for each dataset as these words tend to be comprised of non-noun words such determiner, preposition, etc. which are irrelevant to the candidate keywords for locations.

3.5 Cosine Similarity

For a large document, only counting the maximum common words for similarity measurement sometimes will not work properly. Cosine similarity helps overcome the traditional flaw. It is a well known metric to measure the similarity between different text. Cosine similarity calculates the cosine angle between two vectors to measure the similarity between them.

If $\vec{w}_1$ and $\vec{w}_2$ are two word vectors, then the cosine distance between them is calculated as:

$$cos(\theta) = \frac{\vec{w}_1 . \vec{w}_2}{||\vec{w}_1|| \ ||\vec{w}_2||} \tag{1}$$

where dot (.) indicates dot product and $||\vec{w}_1||$ and $||\vec{w}_2||$ are the length of the vector $\vec{w}_1$ and $\vec{w}_2$ respectively.

Finally, the cosine similarity between $\vec{w}_1$ and $\vec{w}_2$ is computed as:

$$\cos(\vec{w}_1, \vec{w}_2) = 1 - cos(\theta) \tag{2}$$

We used Gensim[9] tools to compute the similarity between the words.

3.6 Steps for Location Extraction

The steps used for identifying the candidate terms in an input news article are as follows:

1. Remove the noisy-words from the input text after applying the pre-processing step describe in Sect. 3.2.
2. Generate all the unique tokens T from the result of Step 1.
3. Load the trained word2vec model for the language.
4. Compute the sum of cosine distance ($S = s_1, s_2 \ldots s_n$) for $t_1, t_2 \ldots t_n \in T$, with each of the seed keyword $k_1, k_2 \ldots k_m \in K$ such that:

$$s_j = \sum_{j=1}^{m} t_i.k_j \tag{3}$$

5. Sort the tokens T based on the ranking of the cosine distance (S).
6. If $T <= 200$, select the top 10 from the sorted list else select the top 20.

The evaluation is carried out based on the number of unique location terms in the ground truth reference present on the list of terms (i.e. either in the top 10 or the top 20) generated by the system.

4 Experiment and Results

The dataset collected for each language is subjected to the same architecture described in Sect. 3 separately. The training dataset is used to build the word embedding model for each of the languages separately using word2vec. The word2vec is trained with different values of *window* and *size*. Here, the window represents the maximum distance between the current and predicted word within a sentence and size is the dimensionality of the word vector. During our experiment, the word2vec trained on the *Skip − gram* language model with $window = 5$, $size = 300$ and *learning rate* $= 0.001$ is observed to be an optimal one. A sample of the word2vec model trained on the dataset of Mizo language is shown in Fig. 3. In the sample, we checked the 10 most similar words for the keyword "aizawl" (the capital city of Mizoram), and the generated words are found to be the location names in Mizoram. This result highlights that the vectors of the location are mapped in the same space.

---

[9] https://radimrehurek.com/gensim/.

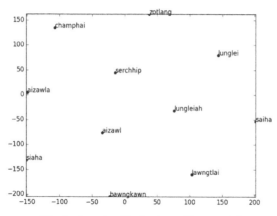

Fig. 3. Sample of trained word2vec model

After training the collected dataset using word2vec, we finally get four word embedding models for each of the languages. We evaluate our proposed model using a test dataset comprising of 20 news article items each on Assamese, English, Manipuri, and Mizo languages separately from the same source as mentioned in Sect. 3.1. The location in each of the news articles from the test dataset is manually tagged by a native or a fluent speaker who also have the domain knowledge about the regions. The annotated dataset is used as our ground truth reference. We employed the steps detailed in Sect. 3 on the test dataset to generate the output. A detailed evaluation of our model is summarized in the Table 2. Table 2 shows the languages followed by the total number of news articles and the combined total number of words in the test dataset, the number of seed keywords used to identify the locations in the input text, the total number of location terms present in the input text (LP), the total number of location terms detected by our model in the test dataset (LD), and recall. The values of recall in Table 2 are in terms of the percentage and is computed as:

$$Recall = \frac{LD}{LP} \times 100 \qquad (4)$$

As shown in Table 2, the model for Mizo language achieve highest accuracy of 92.3% and the model for Assamese language achieve lowest accuracy of 29.7%.

Table 2. Statistics of the output obtained from the model

Language	Articles-words	# Keywords	LP	LD	Recall
Assamese	20–2415	10	47	14	29.7
English	20–5374	7	82	64	78.04
Manipuri	20–6753	7	76	24	31.58
Mizo	20–2312	8	39	36	**92.3**

4.1 Sample Input-Output

A sample input and output for each of the languages is listed below as: the input text in the language, translation to English of the input text, ground truth terms in the input text, and finally the output produced by our system.

Language: Assamese

Input: চৰকাৰী ভূমি বেদখলৰ যেন প্ৰতিযোগিতা চলিছে বটদ্ৰৱাত। বটদ্ৰৱাৰ ভোমোৰাগুৰি গ্ৰেজিং ৰিজাৰ্ভ, বটদ্ৰৱা চৰকাৰী বীজ পাম, শ্ৰীমন্ত শংকৰদেৱ বিশ্ববিদ্যালয়ৰ আৱন্টিত ভূমিৰ কাষৰ চৰকাৰী ভূমি আদি বিভিন্ন চৰকাৰী ভূমি বেদখলৰ বাতৰি প্ৰকাশ পাই থকাৰ সময়তে বটদ্ৰৱা বিধানসভা সমষ্টিৰ অন্তৰ্গত শিলপুখুৰীত চৰকাৰী ভূমি বেদখলৰ অভিযোগ পোৱা গৈছে। প্ৰাপ্ত অভিযোগ অনুসৰি, মৰিগঁাও জিলাৰ মিকিৰৱেটা ৰাজহ চক্ৰৰ অন্তৰ্গত বড়িবজা-ৰস্থিত শিলপুখুৰী গাঁও পঞ্চায়তৰ কাৰ্যালয়ৰ সন্মুখত থকা চৰকাৰী ভূমি যোৱা কিছুদিন ধৰি নিশাৰ ভিতৰতে বেদখল কৰিছে একাংশ দুষ্ট প্ৰকৃতিৰ লোকে।

(*Translation: It seems like a competition is going on to possess govt lands ille- gally at Botodrowa. Amidst the circulation of news on illegal land possession near areas like Botodrowa's Bhomoraguri Grazing Reserve, Botodrowa Government Seed Palm, Srimanta Shankardev University, complaints have been found that there is an illegal possession of government lands at Silpukhuri under Botodrowa legislative assembly. According to the complaint, govt land in front of Silpukhuri Gaon Panchayat, which is situated at Baribazaar area of Marigaon district's Mikirveta Tax Circle, has been illegally possessed by a few miscreants in a matter of days.*)

Ground truth terms in input text: বটদ্ৰৱা, শিলপুখুৰী, মৰিগঁাও
Output: শংকৰদেৱ, অন, মৰিগঁাও, ৰাজহ, নিশাৰ, চক, শিলপুখুৰী, ভূমিৰ, বীজ, টিত

Language: English
Input: A family was poisoned after consuming wild mushrooms. Three persons from Sihai Khullen of Ukhrul district passed away after consuming a mushroom which is locally known as "Ngatha Var." The deceased includes a 70 year old man and his two grandchildren. According to information culled from the villagers, the deceased persons have been identified as Joseph Khangrah, 70; Puimi Khangrah, 5, daughter of Vareiso Khangrah; and Chalakmi Khangrah, 3, son of Vareiso Khangrah. Vareiso Khangrah, father of two deceased children and his wife, Timnah Khangrah along with one of his daughters, Wongayung Khangrah were admitted for medical treatment at RIMS along with some of his relatives who also tasted the dish. They are out of danger and have been discharged from RIMS. As per information made available, the family prepared the mushroom dish on July 2 last for their dinner. After consuming, they vomited but they did not seek medical treatment thinking it would be okay. Joseph Khangrah died on the morning of July 8 after complaining of stomach problems. Chalakmi Khangrah died on the evening of July 10 while Puimila Khangrah died on the way to Imphal after crossing Lambui at around 9:00 pm of July 11. She was advised and referred to go to Imphal by doctors at Ukhrul District Hospital. It may be mentioned here that Sihai Khullen is situated about 37 km from Ukhrul headquarter; and the village falls under Khangkhui Primary Health Centre (PHC), which is much farther away from Ukhrul District Hospital.

The connectivity road is in a pathetic condition which has caused villagers to face a lot of hardships especially during rainy season and availing basic medical treatment.
Ground truth terms in input text: Sihai Khullen, Ukhrul, Imphal, Lambui **Output:** ukhrul, headquarter, district, lambui, khangkhui, khullen, sihai, situated, imphal, phc
Language: Manipuri

Input:তমেংলোং ডিষ্ট্রিক্ট কন্ট্রেক্টরস এসোসিয়েসনগী প্রসিডেন্ট ওইবা স্পিসিয়েল কন্ট্রেক্টর কলানচুং কামেবু এনএসসিএন-আইএম, জেলিয়াংরোং রিজনগী কাংবুনা তমথীবা মওংদা ওত্ নৈরকপা থৌওংবু থোংওংবু এসোসিয়েসন অসিনা অকনবা মওংদা কণেম তৌরক্লি। ঙরাং হেল্ঠ মিনিষ্টর পিঞ্চ পরিজাতুকি তমেংলোং খোঙচত্ মনুংদা ডিষ্ট্রিক্ট হোস্পিটাল, তমেংলোংগী কমপ্লেক্সতা মীটিং চখরিঙৈ নুংথিল পুং 2.30 রোম তাবদা কলানচুং কামেবু এনএসসিএন-আইএমগী জেলিয়াংরোং রিজনগী সিইও লোংচাইবি গোনমৈনা ঙারী অমা শান্নবা পাম্মী হায়-দুনা লুপ অসিগী কাডর অমনা কৌথোকখিবনি হায়রি । কলানচুং কামেবু জিপসি অমগী মনুংদা নমশিনখি অমসুং সিএওগী ওফিসতা পুখি অদুগা সিও জেলিয়াংরোং রিজন এনএস-সিএন আইএমনা কৌবদা লাক্তে অমসুং নবেম্বর মঙাদা হেল্ঠ মিনিষ্টরগী ওফিস চেম্বরদা পাঙথোকখিবা মীটিং অমদা এনএসসিএন-আইএম জেলিয়াংরোং রিজনবু ইকায়বা পীখি হায়না মরাল শীরকপদা মহাক্কা যাদবগী মমিত্-মমায় পুন্শিল্লগা পুং অমা মখায়রোম মীনুংশি হৈতনা চৈনা পংফুদা ফুদুনা ওত্ নৈরকখিবনি হায়রি । অসিগুম্বা থৌওং অসি মতুংদা অমুক হন্না চখদনবসু এসোসিয়েসন অসিনা মরী লৈনবা পুষ্মমক্তা আপিল তৌরক্লি।

(Translation: Tamenglong district contractor's association condemned the ha rassment and illtreatment of its president, special contractor Kalanchung Kamei by NSCN (IM) Jeliangrong region. Yesterday, during the health minister PH. PARIJAT tamenglong visit and an ongoing meeting inside the district hospital at around 2:30 p.m; Kalanchung Kamei was called out by the cadre of NSCN (IM) as he wanted to talk by its (C.O.) Longchaibi Gonmei. Kalanchung Kamei was dumped in a jipsy and carried away to the office of C.A.O, then he was blamed for not coming to the call of C.A.O. Jeliangrong region NSCN (IM) and also on 5th November in the office chamber of health minister. He make ashamed the NSCN (IM) Jeliangrong region, but he denied the charges, then after blindfolded he was beaten mercilessly for about half an hour. So, the association appeal to all not to repeat such acts in the future.)

Ground truth terms in input text: তমেংলোং, জেলিয়াংরোং রিজন
Output: তমেংলোং, কাংবুনা, মঙাদা, ওফিস, জেলিয়াংরোং, পুখি, জিপসি, সিও, রিজনগী, রিজন
Language: Mizo
Input: Mizoram Treasury Accounts Service Association (MITASA) chuan nimin khan Hotel Regencyah inkhawmpui an hmang. Khawzawl, Hnahthial leh Saituala Treasury Office sorkarin hawn a tum chu lawmawm an tih thu an tarlang a, "Chutih rualin, Mizoram Treasury hi siamṭhat (restruct) a ngai a, hei hi remchangah sorkar hnenah thlen ni se," an ti.

(Translation: Mizoram Treasury Accounts Service Association (MISTA) held their conference yesterday at hotel regency. The association announced that it was happy to hear that khawzawl, hnahthial and saitual treasury will be establish soon by the government. In the meantime, Mizoram Treasury needs to be reconstruct and submit it to the government as soon as possible.)

Ground truth terms in input text: Khawzawl, Hnahthial, Saitual

Output: treasury, mizoram, khawzawl, hnahthial, saituala, hawn, regency, accounts, inkhawmpui, chutih.

The system is able to detect the candidate words of locations at the locality level. One of the limitations of our model is inability to differentiate the ambiguity of terms which is used not only as a location, but also as a person's name, organization name's, etc. The system is also not able to detect the exact total number of locations present in the input text.

5 Conclusion

Tools such as POS tagger helps in improving the application of NER tasks, as most of the entity tag belongs to certain parts of speech such as noun. For a low resource-constrained language, building quality language-specific tools such as the POS tagger is a laborious task as it requires an annotated training corpus. In our work, we build a language-independent automatic extraction of location from news articles using seed keywords from the domain knowledge. Our system doesn't rely on language tools such as POS tagger, but instead is purely based on word embedding and the word similarity measure. We tested the feasibility of our model on three low resource-constrained languages belonging to different language groups and also on the English language. Our model is observed to produce a better result on the English and Mizo language as compared to the other remaining language used in our experiment. From the experiment, we observed that the word embedding model trained on a larger dataset performs better than the one trained on a smaller dataset. For regional languages like Assamese and Manipuri, location extraction is a very strenuous and daring task and suffers from a scarcity of resources. Our system is not able to differentiate the ambiguity behavior where the same word is used as a person's name and also as a location's name. In the future, a more enhanced language-independent model that can detect multiple entities can be explored. The model can also be improved in such a way that it can be measured with better evaluation parameters.

Acknowledgement. The authors appreciate the anonymous reviewers for their valuable and profound comments. The authors wish to express their thanks to Elcy S. Lalropeki and L. Tamphangambi for their assistance in this work.

References

1. Achananuparp, P., Hu, X., Shen, X.: The evaluation of sentence similarity measures. In: Song, I.-Y., Eder, J., Nguyen, T.M. (eds.) DaWaK 2008. LNCS, vol. 5182, pp. 305–316. Springer, Heidelberg (2008). https://doi.org/10.1007/978-3-540-85836-2_29
2. Bentham, J., Pakray, P., Majumder, G., Lalbiaknia, S., Gelbukh, A.: Identification of rules for recognition of named entity classes in mizo language. In: Fifteenth Mexican International Conference on Artificial Intelligence (MICAI), pp. 8–13. IEEE (2016)
3. Church, K.W., Hanks, P.: Word association norms, mutual information, and lexicography. Comput. Linguist. **16**(1), 22–29 (1990)

4. Goldberg, Y., Levy, O.: word2vec explained: deriving Mikolov et al.'s negative- sampling word-embedding method. arXiv preprint arXiv:1402.3722 (2014)
5. Imani, M.B., Chandra, S., Ma, S., Khan, L., Thuraisingham, B.: Focus location extraction from political news reports with bias correction. In: IEEE International Conference on Big Data (Big Data), pp. 1956–1964. IEEE (2017)
6. Islam, A., Inkpen, D.: Semantic text similarity using corpus-based word similarity and string similarity. ACM Trans. Knowl. Discovery Data (TKDD) **2**(2), 10 (2008)
7. Lingad, J., Karimi, S., Yin, J.: Location extraction from disaster-related microblogs. In: Proceedings of the 22nd International Conference on World Wide Web, pp. 1017–1020. ACM (2013)
8. Meetei, L.S., Singh, T.D., Bandyopadhyay, S.: Extraction and Identification of Manipuri and Mizo Texts from Scene and Document Images. In: Deka, B., Maji, P., Mitra, S., Bhattacharyya, D.K., Bora, P.K., Pal, S.K. (eds.) PReMI 2019. LNCS, vol. 11941, pp. 405–414. Springer, Cham (2019). https://doi.org/10.1007/978-3-030-34869-4_44
9. Mihalcea, R., Corley, C., Strapparava, C., et al.: Corpus-based and knowledge-based measures of text semantic similarity. In: AAAI, vol. 6, pp. 775–780 (2006)
10. Mikolov, T., Chen, K., Corrado, G., Dean, J.: Efficient estimation of word representations in vector space. arXiv preprint arXiv:1301.3781 (2013)
11. Nadeau, D., Turney, P.D., Matwin, S.: Unsupervised named-entity recognition: generating gazetteers and resolving ambiguity. In: Lamontagne, L., Marchand, M. (eds.) AI 2006. LNCS (LNAI), vol. 4013, pp. 266–277. Springer, Heidelberg (2006). https://doi.org/10.1007/117 66247_23
12. Sharma, P., Sharma, U., Kalita, J.: The first steps towards Assamese named entity recognition. In: Brisbane Convention Center, vol. 1, pp. 1–11 (2010)
13. Singh, T.D., Bandyopadhyay, S.: Web based Manipuri corpus for multiword ner and reduplicated MWEs identification using Svm. In: Proceedings of the 1st Workshop on South and Southeast Asian Natural Language Processing, pp. 35–42 (2010)
14. Singh, T.D., Nongmeikapam, K., Ekbal, A., Bandyopadhyay, S.: Named entity recognition for Manipuri using support vector machine. In: Proceedings of the 23rd Pacific Asia Conference on Language, Information and Computation, vol. 2, pp. 811–818 (2009)
15. Wang, Z., Mi, H., Ittycheriah, A.: Sentence similarity learning by lexical decomposition and composition. arXiv preprint arXiv:1602.07019 (2016)
16. Wen, Y., Yuan, H., Zhang, P.: Research on keyword extraction based on word2vec weighted textrank. In: 2nd IEEE International Conference on Computer and Communications (ICCC), pp. 2109–2113. IEEE (2016)

Uncovering Data Warehouse Issues
and Challenges in Big Data Management

Rohit Kr Batwada$^{(\boxtimes)}$, Namita Mittal$^{(\boxtimes)}$, and Emmanuel S. Pilli$^{(\boxtimes)}$

Malaviya National Institute of Technology, Jaipur, India

`{2017rcp9070,nmittal.cse,espilli.cse}@mnit.ac.in`

Abstract. With the Advancement in Information & Communication Technology, there is an enhancement in Cloud based systems & mobile devices. With the increasing availability & usages of those device, huge data is flowing through various communication channels through different data sources. New demand from academic & industry includes analyzing generated data effectively to come up with fruitful insights that can be actionable either by systems or by humans. Main Goal is to go beyond the questions 'what is happening' and 'why it has happened' to those such as 'what is needed in the future' and 'what are the recommended actions'. Data Lake, which is an extent to Data Warehouse & doing a great job in managing Big Data, providing answers to known questions. In this Paper we are describing issues with traditional data warehouse systems and challenges while managing Big Data with such systems. Also various challenges identified which occurs while understanding the interconnected Data stories in various Data repository and to prepare them for advanced analytics. A novel Data Lake architecture which could work as a Decision support system for Big Data Management has been provided after comparing with other existing.

Keywords: Big Data · Data Lakes · Data Warehouse · Data discovery · Data analysis · Metadata Management

1 Introduction

Human-beings started storing information long back but there was no true relation between the datasets that's how the relation database system came into existence. In the 19th century where people adhered to Mainstream Relational database management systems (RDBMS), entering into the 20th century where the volume & variety of data grew, people started realizing that, their database would not help them to make better decisions and that's where the Data warehouse & BI (Business intelligence) tools came into the picture. Big Data, which has laid down the foundation of all the mega trends happening around us from social to mobile to the cloud to everything. Now, looking at the future, where the emergence of various data sources & "Big Data", brings the demand of Data Lake. *Data lake is emerging as a great asset for any organization due to the huge data which is generating at a faster pace.*

With the advancement of Big Data Management, Data lake which is a considerable prospect as a flexible repository as compared to Data warehouse. The term 'Data Lake'

© Springer Nature Switzerland AG 2020
R. Patgiri et al. (Eds.): BigDML 2019, CCIS 1317, pp. 48–59, 2020.
https://doi.org/10.1007/978-3-030-62625-9_5

itself depicts a 'reservoir, only for Data' [1]. Raw, unstructured data has been kept in a Data Lake in its original format. We need a system, it could be a flat file system where data is moved for processing. Generally Hadoop File System which has already gained popularity due to its speedy processing with huge data sets in the Big Data ecosystem, Data lake is most filled into it to being used.

Due to Data Lake's capability to support storing data in native format, the benefit is, if we have everything to get all known and unknown facts, known facts is being used today but may be things which might not be valuable currently could be turned out interesting in the near future. Adding more to it, Data Flow is exponentially increasing and we never know, data which we lose, will never be captured again so better to make that proof as a future aspect as compared to traditional Data warehouses.

2 Motivation and Background

There are various ways to store Big Data where data storage & data analysis plays an important role to categorise the business use case.

The origin of the project proposal is based on the research article published by the IEEE Computer Society in one of its Journal IEEE Intelligent Systems [1] where Daniel E. O'Leary, compares with existing Enterprise data warehouse (EDW). Investigation using various applications with comparison of Data Lake & Data warehouse has been in place where data sources those required to be integrated from various data sources, facilitating them with Data management.

James Serra, big data and data warehousing solution architect at Microsoft, shares his vision towards using Data Lake over Data warehouse, which also gives the clear directions to think about beyond existing traditional databases systems [2].

Another opinion behind working on Data lake is in industries there is a need to get a 360° view of customer so that business can be improved in multiple ways. Hence there are lot much to explore in Data lake & to deep dive to create such a platform which can extend a Data warehouse Capabilities to meet with Modern day needs. Such platforms are high in demand at domestic as well as international level to store, manage and analyze a variety of data. A new Data Lake architecture approach has been proposed which takes care of issues associated with the Existing Data Warehouses & challenges with existing Data Lake Solutions.

2.1 Data Warehouse and Data Lake

Data warehouses, enormously, a great set of management system to store specially structured data, cleaned up the data & to keep things organised for all business needs. It serves the data for Data Integration & Business Intelligence tools for all their purposes. But now with the addition of various Big Data sources, to make them enable to store all structured & unstructured data in their original form, Data Lake work as a middle layer before data moves into Data warehouse in its structured format (Fig. 1).

It's time for turning data into a service over cloud based platform, hence the questions is quite clear to choose between data warehouse & data lake or else use them together considering data movement flexible from one system to another keeping business analysis on priority (Table 1).

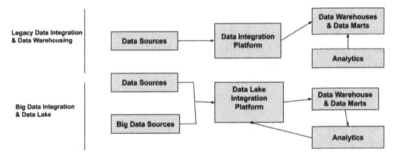

Fig. 1. Data Warehouse & Data Lake design concept

Table 1. Comparison in between Traditional Data warehouse & Modern Data Repository (Data Lake)

Data Warehouse	Data Lake
Data structured in Heavily structured Schemas	Data Structured as is (structured, semi-structured & Unstructured formats)
Pre-Processed data ingestion	Data ingestion is quite rapid
Retails Structured Data	Retains all data
Rigid: hard to Change	Agile : Relatively Easy to Change
Expensive and proprietary	Cheap & open source
Schema-on-load to support historical reporting	Scheme-on-query to support the rapid data exploration & hypothesis testing
Matured in terms on Security	Maturing
Users are likely to be Business Professionals	Data Scientists
Accurate results of past events and performance	'Good Enough' prediction of future events & performance

Whenever there is a debate on both the repositories, Data lake vs data warehouse, which is right for me?, *Few Organizations often need both but in the future,* when all small and medium organization will be facing the Big Data related Challenges, Data lakes which is born out of the need to harness big data and benefit from the raw, granular structured and unstructured data is going to be considered as a best fit.

2.2 Big Data and Data Lake

These two terminology Data lakes and big data analytics in the Data space goes along hand in hand. To make a big data application succeed you need at least two things: knowing what (blended) actionable data you need for your desired outcomes and getting the right data to analyze and leverage in order to achieve those outcomes. Big Data is rapidly growing and becoming the best suitable resources for academics & data industries. Curated & refined data helping companies to improve their functions & helping academic organizations to uncover insights with their research work. But as Data which is now a days flows from multiple sources, it is very important to prevent to get converted into Data Silos & Data Swamps.

Data Lake, an architecture which plays an important role here by pooling all data in a central repository. It act as a storage space of Data for data scientists and other business users that can access it for future use. Data Lake & Big Data has shown a great bond together, with the capability of managing larger quantities of Data, open source Hadoop emerged as a great processing platform. In the era where storage cost is decreasing day by day, the main feature of all big data tools & technologies like Spark, Hadoop etc. that storage cost is slightly low if compared with Data Warehouse considering the solutions these tools can provide. There is a huge demand in terms of Managing Big Data Application & with the support of Data Lake it is going to be a great combination for Data Analyst to work on such centralised repositories to get insights for specific domains due to availability of the actual Origin point of Data.

A data lake can be used as a platform where users are allowed to perform various experiments on set of Data models for specific domains. Data Lake can be specific to a domain where Big Data sets generated to that domain can be received in Raw area. Then it send to staging area where with various transformation techniques this could supplied to Data warehouse to produced curated data to get some known value. But both Data Lake & Data warehouses can be optimized for multiple purposes & main goal should be to design a system which suits all level of enterprises need to get the best solution in each possible way.

2.3 Data Warehouse Issues

Since the growth of Traditional Databases, Data warehousing has become a general practice for many businesses. It becomes a very important aspect in the Modern business era & it heavily depends on modern database models like how they support in business development.

Today, Data consolidation is needed at one location from where it can be easily accessible to all business units for analysis purpose. Insights generated from such data can be applied further to improve business process. But there are some challenges identified which needed for improvement on the existing traditional databases & data warehouse systems.

Structuring of Data
Structuring of Data is required considering future needs in mind as we add more & more data into system, structuring of data becomes difficult & its resulting into slow down the processing speed significantly.

Information Driven Analysis
Traditional Data Warehouses driven by the already placed schema. But Now a days there is a need to drive modern data warehousing by the information we provide while writing the data in it. Analysis needs to be done during the early stages of Implementation, where

it should be designed in a way so that data analyst gets enough time on understanding & documenting the business Needs.

Best Selection of Modern Data Warehouse
There is a huge Gap choosing the right set of operational Modern Database for building a data warehouse out of available tools. Choosing a custom warehouse can save time but pre-configured warehouse could save your time from initial configuration. Although selection of Modern Database depends on business Model & specific goals.

End User Expectations: As more and more information added to a data warehouse, end user expect refined results as analysis considering data stored is from Various resources. At the same time performance is definitely decreased when Data Volume Increases & its leading to reduction in Speed & efficiency.

Investment in Data Governance
Information is one of the Major assets for every organization hence it should be monitored closely. Investment on Data governance allows to define task ownership and ensure that data remains consistent and accurate

3   Related Work

Fang [3] research on Data Lake describes the concept of Data lake around Big Data Era. Data Lake is rapidly growing as a way to organize and build the next generation repository to master new big data challenges. Further he shares the key differentiators between Data Lake and Enterprise Data Warehouse. He suggested four model to validate the deployment with the Hadoop. But in terms of Data Lake, support is given to three type of deployment model those are, EDW with Hadoop, Hadoop growing with Data Lake & Data Lake Cloud.

As per the Shahrokni and Soderberg [4] Data lake is a new concept that has the ability to secure, convert and process the data, which make the data can be consumed with speed and value required by the user even though that operation is quite complicated to run. Instead of moving data in a data store, place it into a data lake in its native format. Prieto and Bregon [5] mentioned the primary goal for setting up a data lake to permit ingestion, storage of large amounts of raw data (all formats) for further transformation and integration. Proposed approach emphasizes Data governance considering data quality while continuously tracking Data & Manipulations before delivering the particular analytics.

As per Rusitschka [6], Big data has been considered in the context of its main 3v's volume, velocity, variety including veracity suggested the few attributes of Data Lake Architecture. In the physical form of Data Lake, many servers are using the distributed file system with a layer of Analytics & Data is catalogued on entry as well as during transformation as per need by the data analyst. This approach contrasts with the current traditional ETL methodology whereas rather than going with 'Extract Transform Load', the process could be followed as 'Extract Load & Transform'. This can be achieved with the 'Schema on Read' approach where, Predefined schema is not playing any role data capturing process.

Ahmad F. [7] Proposes, QoS Lake, its architecture for implementing the QaaS (Quality as a service) model in the same line as PaaS and SaaS using big data technologies. For converting it into service model, approach suggested that Quality of Service in Data lake will be supporting in Analytics & emphasized on Prediction, recommendation & knowledge discovery with Security & Defect Tolerant challenge. Maccioni [8], talks about the Data Preparation part where data scientists needed enough "time-to-action" is exceedingly & it becomes worse when big data sets increased for a Data Lake even no metatags are available to associate & those are included in the ingestion pipeline. KAYAK, a Data Management Framework was proposed to accomplish data preparation in a data lake. It works on metadata cataloging, which keeps track of Meta-Information like how datasets are related to each other.

Suriarachchi and Plale [9] works on Data provenance model which refers to records of the inputs & processes that influence data of interest by providing a historical record of the data and its origins. The paper's three main contributions are related to identification of the data management and traceability issues, Second, reference architecture to overcome the challenges associated in Data Provenance. Third, an evaluation of the proposed architecture to reduce the overhead of Data Provenance.

Raju, Mital and Finkelsztein [10] suggested AIR Traffic Management Data Lake, where The Data Lake had a Cloud component running inside Amazon Web Services (AWS). The data inside the Data Lake is divided into Zones Raw, processed & Refined. Russom P. [11] discussed a tool which is built for inspecting & managing data lakes. Motivation behind the tool development was around Schema discovery solution, identify data security issues & discover data curation process. There are few Challenges faced here in terms of improving the accuracy in joins in tables & gaps were found around integration of Users & tasks.

Sabitha and Vijayalakshmi [12], talks about all happenings around Big Data including recent tools, technologies & challenges those occured due to shift from the traditional systems. Further added that, Devices related to IoT, social websites, automated & smart devices considering as a fuel for the explosion of Data in the near future. Ideal purpose of this paper is to share & discussion the opinions of different researchers, all the available tools for Big Data Process including storage, overall management & analytics. Challenges associated with fee specific domains are highlighted.

Surabhi and Ravinarayana [13] discussed about the need of Data Lake in their survey paper where it is mentioned that to handle the Big Data, Database system processing capabilities required to be extended as per the current capacity. The way Data moves & arrives in Variety & velocity, relational databases architecture is not a perfect fit. The concept of Data Lake has been introduced to take up the challenges arise for Big Data Management.

4 Data Lake Potential and Challenges

Whenever in industries or academics, there is a need to capture information about the client interaction, CRM (Customer Relationship Management) Plays a role here. User record all the details regarding Sales prospective, customer feedback and other information in database. In this case predefined tables representing customer & all associated details.

Nowadays, There is a need to store the information first which is gathered from various resources which can provide a 360° view of Customer & businesses. Current traditional databases are not that much capable to store & capture every piece of data which is getting generated is unstructured, semi-structured & structured format.

Main Goal here is to leverage the capabilities of Data Lake Platform which can help to migrate and upgrade from Traditional database systems to upgraded Modern Cloud Based Data Lake services [14, 15].

When we talk about Big Data Management, Data Lake is not only designed based on the Big Data Platform on Hadoop but it should be designed using multiple technologies which can help Data Lake to design & provide sustainability like Data Warehouse while offering all Capabilities like DW and more to make it analytics compatible.

4.1 Challenges

All the organizations whether it is a Government firm or Private firm or Academics, all have started looking & investing in Data Lake Architecture. With the current flow of Big Data in every type of organizations, there is a need felt for the new data strategy around the generated data & analytics.

Based on the need, Data Lake architecture contains four major components: Data Extraction & Ingestion, Metadata Management & Data Storage, Query Processing Management & Data Lake Management including analytics engine. When we consider the design section, it has various Challenges to address those are described as below. In this paper, Challenges related to each & every component of Data Lake is described in brief. Every issue associated with each component is altogether a separate entity.

4.2 Data Ingestion Challenges

To ingest data in a central repository from various different sources like Social Media, IoT Devices, sensors etc. is required to ingest into system. Few Major Challenges highlighted in current set of Traditional Database systems & existing Data Lake applications.

1. Ingestion of Multiple Source Files, as current tools required a Common Format to Insert.
2. Problem occurs while subsequently Change the loaded data (Support for Merging & updating is an issue in Current Big Data Ingestion Tools), scaling up of the Data is altogether a Challenge for Big Data Organizations.
3. Parallelizing the ingestion process.
4. Completeness, Correctness & Consistency of your data in ingestion pipeline.

   a. Scalability while Data Collection.
   b. Need to identify missing tuples.
   c. Improvement in Data Lineage required to validate Data from source to destination.

4.3 Metadata Management Challenges

Metadata management plays an important role in the design of a Data Lake Architecture. Metadata management is required to understand the Data Lineage issues while validating the data quality. It should be efficient enough to extract the meta tags from the data sources & making the raw data meaningful while associating the metadatas with it. There are few challenges associated with Metadata management while designing the Data lake.

1. Proper governance required while applying Metadata Management.
2. Reduce confusion while data gets ingested into repo.
3. Streamline data interpretation.
4. Reduce the level of effort required to integrate and prepare data.

4.4 Transformation and Query Processing Challenges

There are various challenges occurs in data lake while transformation & query processing i.e.:

1. Loading of multiple tables & so row & columns hence loading time increased.
2. Amount of data fetched by query if used voluminous data for reference hence processing gets slow down.
3. Analysing the data involved complex queries, sub queries & business logics, sometimes could cause timeout errors & get fails.

To simplify the transformation & query processing and at the same time the speed of the data processing is the main challenge which needs to be considered while working on Data Lake's query processing & analytics engine.

5 Proposed Data Lake Architecture

All the organizations whether it is a Government or Private firm or Academics Institutes, all have started looking & investing in building an in-house Data Lake. With the current flow of Big Data in every type of organizations, there is a need felt for the new data strategy around the generated data for analytics purposes. As per the capabilities which an integrated data lake can fulfill, it's architecture contains four major components which includes Data Extraction & Ingestion as part of Data Staging, Metadata Management & Data Storage, Query Processing Management & overall Data Lake Management to ensure smooth functioning from One Component to another component.

Functional & Technical scope of the proposed Data Lake covers below main items where each & every process has its own significance.

5.1 Data Ingestion and Capture

In our approach data ingestion would be categorised in two steps Extraction of Data & Loading of Data.

In Data Lake priority remains as to keep this automated as there are a lot of overheads when companies perform the task to convert incoming data into single or standardized format manually. So for data lake architecture, in this approach, derived models would be based on a platform which can perform the automation of the process along with conducting other tasks like data quality check of the incoming data by managing the overall data ingestion life.

5.2 Storage and Metadata Management for Various Data Formats

Metadata management if effective, becomes the integral art of any data lake. Data lake handled various types of data but there is a huge changes of converting that data into data swamps. Efficient metadata management of any Data warehouse/Data store & Data Lake needs to be capable enough to capture data about data. It would supports during data conversion from Raw data to refined data in proposed data lake.

5.3 Data Processing and Transformations

Data Processing part in proposed approach will take the data input from the Ingestion section, then after processing the data & this will get stored & there are some ways to keep that data in partitioned way.

As per Fig. 2 mechanism need to define where Raw data can be stored to make Data lake meaningful by capturing the origin point of data. Also along with it will keep curated data as well for analytics purpose.

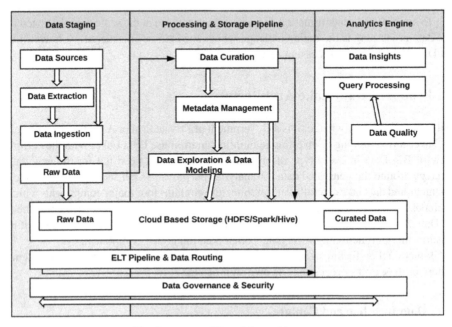

Fig. 2. Proposed Data lake architecture.

5.4 Workflow Management and Scheduling

Workflow management & scheduling refers here for ELT pipeline where after extraction, data gets loaded & then transformed. Main Job here in this step to execution of this pipeline with proper scheduling.

5.5 Data Discovery and Preparation

With Data discovery solution, data lake can be leveraged with adding compatibility for better understanding of data relationships & overall data modeling which would be used for data analysis & if prepared well, data discovery solution module can act as a guide for advanced analytics function for a Data Lake.

5.6 Analytics

Query Processing can be part of the data discovery or analytics section where the soulful purpose of Data lake is to get meaningful insights from the data which gets load in the data lake.

5.7 Data Governance and Data Quality

With Data Quality measures, if data policies, governor limits identified for any data lake, a lot of existing challenges of converting data units into data swamp can be reduced. Whenever there is no existing assurance & strategy about data accuracy & data quality, trust would not be able to generate hence an effective data governance would be needed for any data lake.

6 Discussion

An extensible Data Lake Framework for Big Data Management, handling existing issues will be the key outcome of this Project. This Data Lake Framework will be able to manage structured, semi structured & unstructured Data. It will provide ingestion mechanism, providing a way to use & enrich the metadata with schema designs specific to Domains. It will have a unique storage mechanism which can be a boon for capturing Raw Data as well as Curated Data along with Data Quality. Data governance will also be covered here with basic security & provenance mechanisms. Query Processing & response mechanism from such centric repository will be used for insightful actions.

7 Conclusions and Future Work

A Single Data Store for all Raw Data that anyone could need for analysis could be a great idea to achieve success for Big Data Management. By looking at the needs of a centric data repository organisation has started creating their in- house Data Lakes, but this has not been standardized yet. There are few existing frameworks like Kylo, Zaloni's Data lake etc. are already stepped in the market & few other Kayak, Constance, CoreKG are the research based Frameworks those are yet to get standardised. All Components have a wide scope to work upon in the future. Data Ingestion, Metadata Management, Query Processing on Modern Data Bases & analytics on Data Lake Repository all has wide scope all around. We will limit our approach to a unique mechanism to ingest the data, to provide metadata tagging along with data curation process followed with Query Processing with Great Data Quality parameters.

In Future New Approach those acknowledge the challenges of volume, velocity, and variety towards society is going to be a great step. Lot of Proposals are already in the pipeline relevant to use of Data Lake into various segments of society like Healthcare Management, Smart City Planning, Crime Investigations, Export/Import of the items on which countries are heavily dependant on other countries but can mitigate the gap with proper planning based on investigations needed on available resources. Scientific community actually facing lot of Challenges with the Current Databases systems, in contrast to that available Modern Databases are not fulfilling all the needs.

References

1. O'Leary, D.: Embedding AI and crowdsourcing in the big data lake. IEEE Intell. Syst. **29**, 70–73 (2014)
2. Serra, J.: Why use a data lake?. https://www.jamesserra.com/archive/2015/12/why-use-a-data-lake/
3. Fang, H., Zhang, Z., Wang, C., Daneshmand, M., Wang, C., Wang, H.: A survey of big data research. IEEE Network **29**, 6–9 (2015)
4. Shahrokni, A., Soderberg, J.: Beyond information silos challenges in integrating industrial model-based data. In: CEUR Workshop Proceedings, vol. 1406, pp. 63–72 (2015)
5. Martinez-Prieto, M., Bregon, A., Garcia-Miranda, I., Alvarez-Esteban, P., Diaz, F., Scarlatti, D.: Integrating flight-related information into a (Big) data lake. In: 2017 IEEE/AIAA 36th Digital Avionics Systems Conference (DASC) (2017)
6. Rusitschka, S., Curry, E.: Big data in the energy and transport sectors. In: Cavanillas, J.M., Curry, E., Wahlster, W. (eds.) New Horizons for a Data-Driven Economy, pp. 225–244. Springer, Cham (2016). https://doi.org/10.1007/978-3-319-21569-3_13
7. Ahmad, F., Sarkar, A., Debnath, N.: QoS lake: challenges, design and technologies. In: 2017 International Conference on Recent Advances in Signal Processing, Telecommunications & Computing (SigTelCom) (2017)
8. Maccioni, A., Torlone, R.: Crossing the finish line faster when paddling the data lake with KAYAK. Proc. VLDB Endow. **10**, 1853–1856 (2017)
9. Suriarachchi, I., Plale, B.: Crossing analytics systems: a case for integrated provenance in data lakes. In: 2016 IEEE 12th International Conference on e-Science (e-Science) (2016)
10. Raju, R., Mital, R., Finkelsztein, D.: Data lake architecture for air traffic management. In: 2018 IEEE/AIAA 37th Digital Avionics Systems Conference (DASC) (2018)
11. Russom, P.: Data lakes purposes, practices, patterns, and platforms. https://info.talend.com/rs/talend/images/WP_EN_BD_TDWI_DataLakes.pdf
12. Sabitha M.S., Dr. Vijayalakshmi, R.M., Rathikaa, S.R.E.: Big data – literature survey. IJRASET (2015)
13. Hedge, S.D., Ravinarayana: Survey paper on data lake. Int. J. Sci. Res. **5**, 1718–1719 (2016)
14. Karambelkar, H.: Scaling Big Data with Hadoop and Solr, 2nd edn. (2015)
15. Hegde, S.D., Ravi Narayana, B.: Survey paper on data lake. Int. J. Sci. Res. **5**(7), 2319–7064 (2016)

16. Meena, D., Meena, V.: Data lakes - a new data repository for big data analytics workloads. Int. J. Adv. Res. Comput. Sci. **7**(5) (2016)
17. Huang, P., Chen, Yi.: Enhancing the data privacy for public data lakes. In: Proceedings of IEEE International Conference on Applied System Innovation, pp. 1065–1068 (2018). 978-1-5386-4342-6
18. Zuo, C., Shao, J., Liu, J.K., Wei, G.: Constance: an intelligent data lake system. IEEE Trans. Inf. Forensics Secur. **13**, 186–196 (2018)
19. Klettke, M., Awolin, H., Storl, U., Muller, D., Scherzinger, S.: Uncovering the evolution history of data lakes. In: 2017 IEEE International Conference on Big Data (Big Data) (2017)
20. Amado, A., Cortez, P., Rita, P., Moro, S.: Research trends on Big Data in Marketing: a text mining and topic modeling based literature analysis. Eur. Res. Manage. Bus. Econ. **24**, 1–7 (2018)
21. Kaur, N., Sood, S.: Efficient resource management system based on 4Vs of big data streams. Big Data Res. **9**, 98–106 (2017)

Intrusion Detection in Ad Hoc Network Using Machine Learning Technique

Mahendra Prasad[1(✉)], Sachin Tripathi[1], and Keshav Dahal[2]

[1] Department of Computer Science and Engineering, Indian Institute of Technology (Indian School of Mines), Dhanbad, India
je.mahendra@gmail.com, var_1285@yahoo.com
[2] School of Computing, Engineering and Physical Sciences, University of West of Scotland, Paisley, UK
Keshav.Dahal@uws.ac.uk

Abstract. Ad hoc network is a temporary self-organizing and infrastructure less network. So, it is mostly applied in the military field and disaster relief. Due to wireless communication and self-organizing property ad hoc network is more vulnerable to several intrusions or attacks than the traditional system. Blackhole attack is an important routing disruption attack that malicious node advertises itself as part of a path to the destination. In this paper, we have simulated blackhole attack in ad hoc network environment and collected data of essential features for attack behaviors classification. Then, many machine learning techniques have applied for classification of benign and malicious packet information. It suggests a new approach for select features, essential information collection, and intrusion detection in ad hoc network using machine learning techniques. We have shown comparative results of different machine learning techniques. Our results indicate that this approach can use with different classifiers and can extend it with other intrusions.

Keywords: Intrusion detection · Blackhole attack · Ad hoc network · Machine learning

1 Introduction

In present day, an ad-hoc network has been employed in many applications such military field, disaster relief, and other emergency services [1]. It is a peer-to-peer network that successfully transfers packets through multi-hop without any infrastructure. Due to dynamic nature, ad hoc network requires a unique security scheme to protects the network and detects intrusions or attacks. A popular routing dispersion attack method is known as blackhole attack that contains malicious nodes. These advertise them self as a part of the destination node and try to engage many possible connections [2]. A conventional approach of blackhole provides some solutions that are (1) find more than one routes and send packets, (2) unicast ping packets to the destination using these routes [3]. Intrusion Detection System (IDS) is a popular detection method that detects attacks. It enlarged the detection capacity and decreased the false alerts. An IDS can detect any violation

© Springer Nature Switzerland AG 2020
R. Patgiri et al. (Eds.): BigDML 2019, CCIS 1317, pp. 60–71, 2020.
https://doi.org/10.1007/978-3-030-62625-9_6

of security policies such as confidentiality, authenticity, integrity and availability [4]. A detection method can classify into benign and attacks by employing Machine Learning (ML) technique. There are many ML algorithms exist with pros and cons depend on nature of dataset. The ML works on learning method whether supervised, unsupervised or semi-supervised [5]. We have enumerated our major work below.

1. A blackhole attack is simulated in Network Simulator (NS-3) with many normal and malicious nodes. Where a malicious node can accommodate its all malicious activities.
2. We have analyzed the main features of the node and collected essential information of packets or message sending by nodes and organized them.
3. Finally, ML techniques have applied in the supervised mode of training on the collected data to detect malicious information or packets and measured their performance.

The rest of paper is arranged in the following sequence. Section 2 reviews recent literatures and Sect. 3 elaborates key topics as preliminaries, while Sect. 4 discuss proposed methodology. In Sect. 5, it descries simulation of the proposed method. Section 6 provides performance measures and comparative results. Finally, we conclude proposed method and future direction in Sect. 7.

2   Related Work

An IDS is a quick monitoring system and produce an alert when finding any intrusion. In this section, mainly introduce detection methods which related to IDS in ad hoc network. Kalkha et al. [6] proposed an approach based on a new routing algorithm to identify and avoid malicious node in the wireless sensor network. They applied the Hidden Markov Model to identify the most likely malicious path and detection module analyses the shortest path from source to destination. Omar et al. [7] proposed a threshold based multi-hop acknowledgment method that considered as blackhole node when the reputation of node increase or decrease to the threshold. Chatterjee et al. [8] suggested triangular encryption due to its low computation overhead and simulated it in network simulator NS-2. Panos et al. [9] proposed a dynamic threshold cumulative sum based mechanism that detects abrupt changes in normal behavior.

Mitrokotsa et al. [10] described a model selection and classification method for intrusion detection in ad hoc network. They had worked on selected features which are RREQ Sent, RREQ Received, RREP Sent, RREP Received, RERR Sent, RERR Received, Data Sent, Data Received, Number of Neighbors, PCR (Percentage of change in route entries) and PCH (Percentage of change in number of Hop). They also analyzed the cost and effect of the model. Subsequently, examined tuning of classifiers when unknown attacks appear in the system. They shown approx 90% detection rate vs FN to FP cost and approx 05% false alarm rate vs FN to FP cost of blackhole attack. Sen et al. [4] introduced an IDS using an evolutionary technique in ad hoc network. They have explored evolutionary computation techniques specifically genetic programming and grammatical evaluation. Then, employed multi-objective evolutionary technique to discover optimal trade-off.

Feng et al. [11] proposed an IDS method for anomalies detection in ad hoc network based on the learning method. They have applied deep learning to detect Denial-of-Service (DoS) and privacy attacks by grab packet information in ad hoc network. Subba et al. [12] proposed hybrid IDS in ad hoc network for unsupervised data. Their method elect cluster leader that provides intrusion detection service. Hybrid IDS comprises a lightweight and heavyweight module that detects intrusions and incomplete information anomalies. These works are simulated in network simulator and applied machine learning techniques to detect intrusions. We have proposed ML-based detection method and demonstrated a promising effect against blackhole attack in ad hoc network.

3 Preliminaries

3.1 Ad Hoc Network

Ad hoc is an infrastructure less and temporary self-organizing network. It establishes for special services such as battlefield, rescue services, etc. where no preexisting infrastructure or infrastructure failed [10, 11]. The application of this network is dynamic nature and quickly deployed. It is composed of nodes at different places and transfers messages to nodes in radio range. Neighbor nodes in network help for transferring message from source to destination [4, 12] using a routing protocol. Ad hoc On-demand Distance Vector (AODV) comes under distance vector routing protocols and applies in ad hoc network. AODV uses Route-Request (RREQ) packets when a node requires to build a route towards the destination. An immediate node sends RREQ to neighbors in range and establish a route and answers the source node by Route-Reply (RREP) packet. Due to the mobility of node every new diffusion establish a route [13]. A dynamic nature in the wireless environment of network intruders can easily adapt.

3.2 Blackhole Attack

Blackhole attack contains malicious nodes that can engage data packets by a false route reply packet. Malicious nodes falsely claim that have shortest route to the destination. When they receive data packets simply drop them. A malicious node tries to engage as a much possible active connection to the network resources. When the source establishes a malicious route node sends a false route reply message and acknowledge that it has an active route to the destination node [2, 14]. A conventional method suggests mitigating blackhole attack in ad hoc network. Unlike other approaches detect malicious node after the carried out information while some approach identified malicious nodes before the routing process and isolate them [14]. Our aim to detect malicious information during the routing process using the ML technique in ad hoc network. Then, it sends an alert to the network administrator.

3.3 Machine Learning Techniques

Despite the improvement of security schemes, continuous changing attack methods that need robust detection technique. The most acceptable technique is detecting in the context of attack sample whether the sample is normal or malicious. When analyzes sample is malicious then isolate it before harm network resources [5]. The whole detecting process is based on learning method that can learn by a group of sample then provide a decision. ML techniques have been categorized into three categories which are supervised, unsupervised, and semisupervised learning. These are adopted by ML techniques that are applied to detect blackhole attack in this work. We have simulated many ML techniques on blackhole attack samples such as Ada Boost, Bayes Net [15], Decision Table, Hoeffding Tree, J48, KStar, Multi-Layer Perceptron (MLP) [16], Naive Bayes [15], Random Forest, Random Tree, and Stochastic Gradient Descent (SGD) [17]. These ML techniques work in only labeled dataset or supervised mode of training.

MLP is more suitable for linearly separable binary class problem [16]. It consist with minimum three layer namely input layer, hidden layer, and output layer. Naive Bayes and Bayes Net classifier are effectively used for condition monitoring that can applied for multi class [15]. SGD addresses the problem of high computational cost by some modification in gradient decent algorithm. It is only differ by how much data compute gradient for objective function and much faster convergence [17].

3.4   Intrusion Detection System

An IDS is immediate detecting method by intruders carry out information against the system. The primary aim to detect intrusions in communication and generate an alert to network administrator [11]. This is a powerful system to detect malicious information in the learning mode of training. Traditionally, intrusion was detected by conventional approaches such as encryption and decryption, authentication, firewall, etc. It is categorized in three categories such misuse detection system, anomaly detection system, and hybrid detection system. A misuse detection system is executed by matching the sample which is stored in the database and provide the decision. Anomaly detection system checks any deviation of sample form baseline if get then mark as malicious. Hybrid detection system uses both detection method property and reduces the drawback of detection system [13]. It is much powerful detection system than others and gives an acceptable decision.

4   Proposed Method

This section elaborates the proposed method of blackhole attack detection. We assume that the ad hoc network comprises N bidirectional communication nodes in the network space that share packets or information over a shared wireless medium. This network space contains $N - M$ normal nodes and M malicious nodes. Malicious nodes tune their behaviors and perform malicious activities. This method starts with feed data and simulates blackhole attack with malicious nodes. Subsequently, it gathers basic information of nodes which are in ad hoc network in a specified format. Then, this process selects essential features and collect data that build a dataset. Finally, we have applied many ML techniques for classification of information and provided the valid decision. A sequence of work is described in Algorithm 1.

Algorithm 1 Blackhole attack detection

1: input initial coordinate of nodes in the form of X and Y.
2: simulate some nodes with malicious activities as blackhole attack that attracts packet and drops it and others as normal.
3: trace pcap file of each node at each stage of message transfer and receive.
4: export packet informations in required file.
5: select essential features.
6: data collection using selected features.
7: apply various ML techniques to classify normal and malicious information.
8: store outcome as a confusion matrix.
9: compute different statistical measures.
10: evaluate comparative results.

We have described details of simulation procedure such as essential feature selection, data collection process, statistical measures, and different ML techniques results in the next section. It is also shown simulation results and tabled comparative results of ML techniques.

5 Experiments

5.1 Simulation

We have simulated blackhole attack in network simulator NS-3 [18]. Despite of NS-2, it is more priorities the use of the standard tool for input and output of file format therefore external tool also can be used. It is not a purely new simulator but also simulates predecessor simulator concepts, program, and data. The NS-3 provides network simulation in C++ and python program. To execute this work, the simulator enters into the main loop that executes events in predefined order from the data structure. This process continues until the event stack empty or predefined time has reached. In this simulation, network contains 25 nodes in network space including five malicious nodes. Experimental parameters of the simulator environment are topology space 1000 × 1000 m2, random node movement, radio range 250 m, etc. Figure 1 shows nodes position and radio range at a stage of nodes communication.

In recent days, WEKA (Waikato Environment for Knowledge Analysis) is recognized as a landmark system of data mining and ML. It allows researchers easy access to state-of-the-art technology in ML [19] and it has explored learning algorithms in many languages on various platforms which can operate on different types of data formats. WEKA is not only providing a toolbox of learning algorithms but also provides a framework for researchers can deploy a new learning algorithm. The task of WEKA is collecting dataset and providing results on selected ML techniques would be in various statistical parameters. We have executed our collected dataset on 11 different ML algorithms under 10-fold cross-validation and analyzed comparative results.

5.2 Data Generation

We have traced the output (Packet Capture in short pcap) files which have enough information to compute the required parameters. Any publicly available tool can analyze

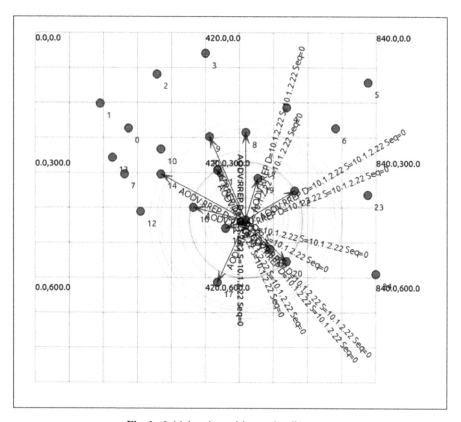

Fig. 1. Initial node position and radio range.

*.pcap traces file and gathers information for the further process. NS-3 supports standard output format for traced data which is in pcap format. We have used Wireshark and tcpdump [18] packet analysis tool to export data into standard or required file format.

5.3 Features Detail

It is a difficult task to select features that distinguish normal node and malicious node information. Features may depend on network structure and mode of data transmission. This work has analyzed the whole characteristics of nodes and gathered information into a proper format. A continuous data type provides simple information as numbers, and discrete data type may provides the string information.

From Table 1, duration indicates the transferring time of the packet from source to destination. The flag shows the status of packets and hopcount shows the intermediate nodes. Size of packets defines in packet size that includes header length in themselves. Messages are divided into many categories which are mainly Route Request, Route Reply, Route Acknowledgment, etc. Neighbor node is a number of node surrounding the node in communication range. When the sender and originator of message are same, then land indicates by Zero otherwise One. Unicast and broadcast are two different types of message transferring modes. Message sequence number, originator sequence number, and stream index are generated sender or receiver for uniquely identified packets. The flow of message through the nodes can define the highest flow, lowest flow, average flow. Number failed connection and failure rate can compute using the Route Error message.

Table 1. Information of adopted features to aim of blackhole attack detection

S.No.	Feature name	Type
1	Duration	Continuous
2	Protocol	Discrete
3	Packet size	Continuous
4	Flag	Discrete
5	Header length	Continuous
6	Hop count	Continuous
7	Life time	Continuous
8	Message type	Discrete
9	Destination sequence number	Continuous
10	Message transfer mode	Discrete
11	Number of neighbors	Continuous
12	Land	Discrete
13	Message sequence number	Continuous
14	Stream index	Continuous
15	Highest flow	Continuous
16	Average flow	Continuous
17	Lowest flow	Continuous
18	Average hop count	Continuous
19	Number of failed connection	Continuous
20	Failed connection rate	Continuous
21	Label	Discrete

Finally, label the message or sample using the unique id of node generated or transferred message in the network.

5.4 Data Collection

We have collected distinct 711 (80 malicious and 631 benign) samples on 13 basic features including binary labels (named as Dataset-1). A quantity of benign sample is much higher than the malicious sample that can decrease the performance of the system. The size of the dataset is small that can lead the problems like bias or overfitting.

Although, we extend this work by increasing the features and simulation time that provide a new dataset. It contains 12,604 (2,654 malicious and 9,950 benign) samples that have 21 features including binary labels named as Dataset-2.

6 Result Analysis

6.1 Performance Measures

The outcome of the algorithm is collected in the form of confusion matrix that computes different statistical parameters by True Positive (TP), False Positive (FP), True Negative (TN), and False Negative (FN). TP is sample predicted as normal whenever the actual sample is also normal. TN is sample predicted as attack whenever the actual sample is also attack. FN is sample predicted as attack whenever the actual sample is normal. FP is sample predicted as normal whenever the actual sample is attack [11].

$$TPR(Recall) = \frac{TP}{TP + FN} \tag{1}$$

$$FPR = \frac{FP}{FP + TN} \tag{2}$$

$$Precision = \frac{TP}{TP + FP} \tag{3}$$

$$F - measure = \frac{2 * Recall * Precision}{Recall + Precision} \tag{4}$$

$$Accuracy = \frac{TP + TN}{TP + FP + TN + FN} \tag{5}$$

$$Avg.Performance = \sum_{i=1}^{c} \frac{S_i}{S} * Performance_i \tag{6}$$

Where TPR is true positive rate and FPR is the false positive rate. Recall and TPR is the same whenever Precision provides correct prediction by test samples. F-measure provides a harmonic mean of Precision and Recall. Accuracy is the proportion of true prediction and total samples. $S = (S1 + S2 + ... + Sc)$ is the total sample and c is a number of class that computes the average performance of the system.

6.2 Performance Comparison

This section summarizes results of different ML techniques which executed on collected data of blackhole attack in ad hoc network. Table 2 shows results of computed statistical parameters such as TPR, FPR, Precision, F-measure, and accuracy. ML techniques such as Ada Boost, Bayes Net, Decision Table, Hoeffding Tree, J48, KStrar, MLP, Naive Bayes, Random Forest, Random Tree, and SGD are executed on Dataset-1.

Table 2. Performance of machine learning techniques for Dataset-1

Technique	TPR	FPR	Precision	F-measure
Ada Boost	0.931	0.249	0.933	0.932
Bayes Net	0.880	0.223	0.913	0.892
Decision Table	0.956	0.180	0.956	0.956
Hoeffding Tree	0.923	0.512	0.915	0.912
J48	0.951	0.181	0.952	0.951
KStar	0.887	0.538	0.878	0.882
MLP	0.932	0.205	0.938	0.935
Naive Bayes	0.885	0.298	0.904	0.892
Random Forest	0.927	0.271	0.929	0.928
Random Tree	0.907	0.481	0.898	0.901
SGD	0.934	0.205	0.938	0.936

Table 2 shows results on mentioned parameters that can easily recognize the best technique. When an attack is detected in the system then sends an alarm to the network administrator to isolates that node. While FN higher value indicates, normal packet information is falsely predicted as an attack. FP is the opposite of FN which indicates attack falsely detected as normal meanwhile the system allows the attack to enter and harm network resources. Decision Table classifier shows lower FPR and higher TPR, Precision, and F-measure. An opposite of this, KStar technique is shown higher FPR and lower Precision and F-measure. While Naive Bayes technique is shown lower TPR or Recall. Decision Table is producing a better detection system whenever KStar and Naive Bayes both are quantitatively given poor results.

Table 3 shows confusion matrix of SGD, Bayes Net, and MLP of Dataset-2 that use for statistical parameters computation. Table 4, 5 and 6 show the performance on different statistical parameters of SGD, Bayes Net, MLP respectively. The performance of the system is measured with the help of statistical parameters. TP and TN are correct prediction parameters which higher value improve system performance, and lower value decreases the system performance. FP and FN are the incorrect predictions of parameters which lower value improve the performance of the system and higher value decrease the system performance. These parameters are used to compute performance measures such as TPR, FPR, Precision, F-measure, and Accuracy.

Table 3. Confusion matrix for Dataset-2

SGD			Bayes Net			*MLP*		
Class	Benign	Malicious	Class	Benign	Malicious	Class	Benign	Malicious
Benign	9841	2439	Benign	9145	529	Benign	9912	154
Malicious	109	215	Malicious	805	2125	Malicious	38	2500

Table 4. Statistical parameters of SGD for Dataset-2

Parameters	Benign	Malicious	Avg. performance
TP	9841	215	–
TN	215	9841	–
FP	2439	109	–
FN	109	2439	–
TPR	0.989	0.081	0.798
FPR	0.918	0.010	0.728
Precision	0.80	0.664	0.773
F-measure	0.885	0.144	0.730
Accuracy	0.798	0.798	0.798

Table 5. Statistical parameters of Bayes Net for Dataset-2

Parameters	Benign	Malicious	Avg. performance
TP	9145	2125	–
TN	2125	9145	–
FP	529	805	–
FN	805	529	–
TPR	0.919	0.80	0.894
FPR	0.199	0.080	0.174
Precision	0.945	0.725	0.90
F-measure	0.932	0.761	0.896
Accuracy	0.894	0.894	0.894

Table 7 shows performance of detection system where SGD, Bayes Net, MLP are performed on Dataset-2. In these detection systems, MLP provides a higher detection rate, precision, F-measure, accuracy, and lower false alarm rate. The training complexity

Table 6. Statistical parameters of MLP for Dataset-2

Parameters	Benign	Malicious	Avg. performance
TP	9912	2500	–
TN	2500	9912	–
FP	154	38	–
FN	38	154	–
TPR	0.996	0.942	0.985
FPR	0.058	0.004	0.047
Precision	0.984	0.985	0.985
F-measure	0.990	0.963	0.985
Accuracy	0.985	0.985	0.985

of detection systems of Dataset-2 as SGD (0.55 s), Bayes Net (0.15 s), and MLP (1.77 s). MLP took more training time to other ML techniques.

Table 7. Overall performance of detection system for Dataset-2

Classifier	TPR	FPR	Precision	F-measure	Accuracy
SGD	0.798	0.728	0.772	0.730	0.798
Bayes Net	0.894	0.174	0.90	0.896	0.894
MLP	0.985	0.047	0.985	0.985	0.987

7 Conclusion

In this paper, we have proposed a machine learning based intrusion detection system in the ad hoc network where intrusion as a blackhole attack. Blackhole attack is applied in the network and simulated with many malicious nodes. The main features of nodes are identified and collected information of traced pcap file using tcpdump. This information makes a set of distinct samples which is with known labels. Machine learning techniques are applied to this set of data which work in the supervised mode of training. Experiments show the simulated blackhole attack such activities, and various machine learning techniques provide their detection accuracy. Where MLP is shown the better result to other classifiers, it has shown 98.5% detection rate and 4.7% false alarm rate whenever it took more training time. These promising results encourage us to extend this work to identify more useful features and collect more information. Moreover, this work may simulate with other intrusions.

References

1. Khanna, N., Sachdeva, M.: A comprehensive taxonomy of schemes to detect and mitigate blackhole attack and its variants in MANETs. Comput. Sci. Rev. **32**, 24–44 (2019)
2. Khamayseh, Y.M., Aljawarneh, S.A., Asaad, A.E.: Ensuring survivability against black hole attacks in MANETs for preserving energy efficiency. Sustain. Comput. Inform. Syst. **18**, 90–100 (2018)
3. Al-Shurman, M., Yoo, S.-M., Park, S.: Black hole attack in mobile ad hoc networks. In: Proceedings of the 42nd Annual Southeast Regional Conference, pp. 96–97. ACM (2004)
4. Sen, S., Clark, J.A.: Evolutionary computation techniques for intrusion detection in mobile ad hoc networks. Comput. Netw. **55**(15), 3441–3457 (2011)
5. Ucci, D., Aniello, L., Baldoni, R.: Survey of machine learning techniques for malware analysis. Comput. Secur. **81**, 123–147 (2018)
6. Kalkha, H., Satori, H., Satori, K.: Preventing black hole attack in wireless sensor network using HMM. Procedia Comput. Sci. **148**, 552–561 (2019)
7. Hammamouche, A., Omar, M., Djebari, N., Tari, A.: Lightweight reputation-based approach against simple and cooperative black-hole attacks for MANET. J. Inf. Secur. Appl. **43**, 12–20 (2018)
8. Chatterjee, N., Mandal, J.K.: Detection of blackhole behaviour using triangular encryption in NS2. Procedia Technol. **10**, 524–529 (2013)
9. Panos, C., Ntantogian, C., Malliaros, S., Xenakis, C.: Analyzing, quantifying, and detecting the blackhole attack in infrastructure-less networks. Comput. Netw. **113**, 94–110 (2017)
10. Mitrokotsa, A., Dimitrakakis, C.: Intrusion detection in MANET using classification algorithms: the effects of cost and model selection. Ad Hoc Netw. **11**(1), 226–237 (2013)
11. Feng, F., Liu, X., Yong, B., Zhou, R., Zhou, Q.: Anomaly detection in ad-hoc networks based on deep learning model: a plug and play device. Ad Hoc Netw. **84**, 82–89 (2019)
12. Subba, B., Biswas, S., Karmakar, S.: Intrusion detection in mobile ad-hoc networks: Bayesian game formulation. Eng. Sci. Technol. Int. J. **19**(2), 782–799 (2016)
13. Liu, G., Yan, Z., Pedrycz, W.: Data collection for attack detection and security measurement in mobile ad hoc networks: a survey. J. Netw. Comput. Appl. **105**, 105–122 (2018)
14. Woungang, I., Dhurandher, S.K., Obaidat, M.S., Peddi, R.D.: A DSR-based routing protocol for mitigating blackhole attacks on mobile ad hoc networks. Secur. Commun. Netw. **9**(5), 420–428 (2016)
15. Muralidharan, V., Sugumaran, V.: A comparative study of Naïve Bayes classifier and Bayes net classifier for fault diagnosis of monoblock centrifugal pump using wavelet analysis. Appl. Soft Comput. **12**(8), 2023–2029 (2012)
16. Yi-Chung, H.: Pattern classification by multi-layer perceptron using fuzzy integral-based activation function. Appl. Soft Comput. **10**(3), 813–819 (2010)
17. Sharma, A.: Guided stochastic gradient descent algorithm for inconsistent datasets. Appl. Soft Comput. **73**, 1068–1080 (2018)
18. Riley, G.F., Henderson, T.R.: The ns-3 network simulator. In: Wehrle, K., Güneş, M., Gross, J. (eds.) Modeling and Tools for Network Simulation, pp. 15–34. Springer, Heidelberg (2010). https://doi.org/10.1007/978-3-642-12331-3_2
19. Hall, M., Frank, E., Holmes, G., Pfahringer, B., Reutemann, P., Witten, I.H.: The weka data mining software: an update. ACM SIGKDD Explor. Newslett. **11**(1), 10–18 (2009)

Big Data Issues in SDN Based IoT: A Review

Syeda Zeenat Marshoodulla[✉], Rohit Kumar Das, and Goutam Saha

North-Eastern Hill University, Shillong, Meghalaya, India
syeda.zeenat@gmail.com, rohitdas.it.13@gmail.com,
dr.goutamsaha@gmail.com

Abstract. IoT infrastructure is resource and energy constraint. The emergence of a smart world has led to the interconnection of diverse objects with the Internet which leads to the generation of a tremendous amount of data which can be referred to as Big Data. Since the IoT is going to be expanded in a exponential manner, Big Data Issues becomes a threat for its faithful operation. Other than this, the existing IoT architecture has limitations with respect to scalability, reliability, availability, etc. To overcome these limitations along with resolution of Big Data issues, investigators proposed different types of architectures for its improvement. In this paper, we have tried to highlight the evolution of conventional IoT architecture to SDN based IoT architecture which offers better provisions to resolve Big Data issues also. This review paper also highlights the procedures, developed by investigators of the area, as to how Big Data issues can be resolved in these architectures. Further research scopes arising out of the present endeavor are also been highlighted which will provide the direction of future research in the area.

Keywords: Big data · Big Data issues · Data analytics · Internet of Things · Software defined network

1 Introduction

The number of smart devices connecting to the Internet is increasing day by day. This demands the leverage of Big Data analytics processes in order to achieve the full advantage of the services provided by the Internet of Things (IoT). IoT is one of the major sources of generating a huge amount of data [1]. According to Cisco, Machine to Machine (M2M) connections will be more than half of the global connected devices and connections by the year 2022. The share of M2M connections will grow from 34% in 2017 to 51% by 2022 [2]. As the number continues to grow, the problems of collecting such huge amount of data, its analysis and transmission of the same to the cloud for storage becomes more challenging. The real issues concerning Big Data in IoT originated from the resource-constrained configuration of IoT and heterogeneity of the data sources associated with IoT. Moreover, accurate and real-time analysis of the data in the shortest possible time is also necessary for the prompt action of the actuators employed. Proper network utilization should also be considered so that maximum optimization is obtained.

The Big Data issues in conventional IoT system is difficult to resolve as it is resource-constrained. Solutions for Big Data issues requires formidable computational power. This

© Springer Nature Switzerland AG 2020
R. Patgiri et al. (Eds.): BigDML 2019, CCIS 1317, pp. 72–82, 2020.
https://doi.org/10.1007/978-3-030-62625-9_7

is not possible in IoT devices. So, it can be resolved in the Cloud level which may have many difficulties with respect to the commercial point of view, security point of view etc. Therefore, many competing IoT architectures have been proposed to resolve this difficulty along with many other bottlenecks existing in the conventional IoT system. The significant characteristics of IoT data in cloud platforms are briefly mentioned in [3]. A basic conventional architecture of IoT is shown below in Fig. 1.

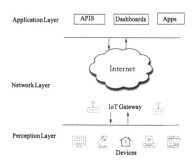

Fig. 1. Simple IoT architecture.

The main difference between conventional and SDN based IoT system is the resource-constrained gateways of IoT system which can be replaced by Controllers [4]. This controllers are powered with more computational resources. So, some of the Big Data issues can be resolved here itself. Big Data issues would become a bit feasible if the conventional IoT system could be upgraded to Software Defined Network (SDN) based IoT. Therefore, resolving Big Data issues in SDN based IoT system has now become a potential research issue both from academia and industry. SDN is a concept which gives a new dimension to the existing network by decoupling the control and the data plane. It has several advantages especially for Big Data analysis of IoT. The conventional networks are increasingly adopting the SDN architecture for its ability to program the network [5].

Data extracted from different environment serves as a very important component in decision-making processes for various Industrial operations. Nowadays, data collected from different sources have increased tremendously including IoT system and it is now in the order of petabytes and zeta bytes in volume. According to a report by the International Data Corporation (IDC), the estimated global data volume will increase by a factor of 300, from 130 EB in 2005 to 40,000 EB in 2020, which amounts to double the growth every two years [6]. Additionally, the nature of this data is of highly complex. It can be safely termed as Big Data. Big Data exhibits some distinct characteristics.

Big Data can be defined by five V's [7] namely-Volume, Velocity, Variety, Veracity and Value. The common processes involved in Big Data utilization is given by Zhang et al. in [8]. With proper analytical tools, time series data can provide valuable insights into the dynamics of the process whose time series data has been that will help in taking precise decisions. IoT system produces Big Data whose solution is becoming very difficult due to a lot of constraints in the IoT system. Table 1 exhibits the difference between conventional data and Big Data.

Table 1. Comparison of Traditional Data and Big Data.

Comparison parameter	Traditional data processing	Big data processing
Rate of data	Slow	Rapid
Storage feasibility format	Feasible structured	Unfeasible
Data source	Mostly centralized	Semi-structured and unstructured
Mode of operation	Interactive/Offline	Fully distributed
Accuracy	Approximate	Batch/Real time
		Accurate

One of the standard methodology to solve Big Data problems is Hadoop based approaches. An open-source platform or framework that serves as a solution to the storage and the processing of Big Data is Apache Hadoop [9]. It runs on clusters of commodity servers that can support the storage and processing of the massive data. The main components of the Hadoop architecture are Hadoop Distributed File System-HDFS, YARN, MapReduce and Hadoop Common [10]. HDFS allows the unstructured as well as structured data to be stored in a distributed fashion across the clusters. It consists of a single Name Node and multiple Data Nodes. YARN performs the necessary resource management tasks such as scheduling jobs. MapReduce consists of the two phases i.e. Map and Reduce phases. In Map phase, data are split into proper format (key/value pairs) and then analyzed to produce sub-results. In the reduce phase, these sub-results are combined to give the final result. Hadoop Common is a set of shared utilities and libraries that provide the underlying capabilities required. Hadoop supports a range of processing frameworks to extend its basic capabilities like Apache Pig, Apache Hive, etc.

Due to the complex characteristics of Big Data, traditional systems are inadequate to handle the huge data sets. The main challenges in the Big Data analysis are storage, transmission, efficient tools and finally presenting the results in proper formats for various decision-making and other tasks. This paper deals with different methodologies adopted by earlier researchers to deal with Big Data problem on the SDN based IoT platform.

The remainder of the paper is as follows. In Sect. 2, an SDN based IoT-Big Data architecture have been examined. In Sect. 3, existing related works are reviewed and analyzed. Section 4 presents the Big Data challenges and issues in the present scenario. Section 5 identifies the future scope in this area. Finally, Sect. 6 concludes the paper.

2   SDN Based IoT-Big Data Architecture

A simple IoT based architecture is shown in Fig. 1. A few SDN based IoT-Big Data analysis architectures can be found in the literature. Figure 1 and Fig. 2 will help in distinguishing the difference between them.

The architecture as shown in Fig. 2 provides an overall abstraction of the system. The Infrastructure layer consists of the IoT layer and the network layer. The sensors and other devices reside in the IoT layer. The Network layer consists of the network elements like routers, switches, etc. The Infrastructure layer is also called the data plane

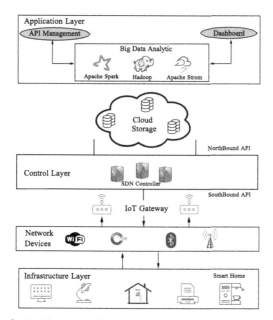

Fig. 2. Architecture of SDN-IoT with big data analytics [6, 11].

for SDN network. The Control layer is placed above the Infrastructure layer that helps to dynamic configuration of the network. The Control layer interacts with the network elements through the South-bound Interface (SBI) [6]. One of the most commonly used SBI protocol used is 'OpenFlow'. The SDN controller can be of either open-source or commercial based such as NOX, POX, FloodLight, Ryu, Open Day Light, Beacon, etc. The Application layer is placed on the top. It consists of various applications and Application Programming Interface (APIs) to direct the network and check its status. The SDN controller interacts with the Application layer using the North-bound Interface (NBI). The Big Data analytics framework resides in the application layer that makes the decision-making process and other complex analytical processes [11]. Big Data application architecture for smart cities using SDN based IoT has been proposed by Din et al. in [12]. It consists of four layers with three main levels and two intermediate levels as shown in Fig. 3.

The smart services like smart home, smart transportation, smart healthcare, etc. produce an enormous amount of data from IoT sensor-embedded devices which are gathered and passed on to the upper layer using the intermediate level i.e. an SDN based network. SDN controller identifies the sensor data, manages the application-based routing as well as check for congestion in a link. At the Data Processing and Management Level, meaningful data can be extracted using a framework like Hadoop Distributed File System to store and manage the data. Cluster-based Hadoop System can be used for processing huge data. Applications such as GraphX and SPARK can be used for real-time data processing.

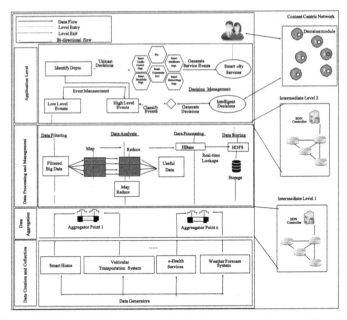

Fig. 3. SDN based IoT architecture for big data analysis in smart cities [12]

3   Literature Review

In this section, some of the current research works and their contributions to address the problems associated with Big Data generated by IoT have been discussed.

Big Data in IoT: A basic mathematical analysis was presented in [13] by Ding et al. to give a practical approach to the Big Data processing in IoT. They have focused on four massive data processing encountering the issues - the heterogeneity of data generated by IoT devices, the non-linear processing of Big Data, the multi-dimensional aspect of data processing and the decentralized and parallel processing of the data. The information will open more practical researches in this direction. The authors of [14] have described the varieties of Big Data generation by IoT and support for localized and real-time analysis can be addressed by the fusion of data which yields better data analysis. Existing data mining algorithms as well as improved clones have proved to be helpful in the Big Data analysis process. In [15], the authors Alam et al. have experimented the applicability of existing data mining algorithms in simpler IoT datasets and has found to have higher accuracy. However, the algorithms were computationally expensive and some investigations are required to reduce it. In [16], the authors Dineshkumar et al. proposed a system of Big Data analysis on health data using Hadoop and map reduce. Big Data analysis in healthcare is of significant importance both for the patient as well as doctors. In [17], the authors Kang et al. presented an implementation model of RFID/sensor data repository using MongoDB, which is a popular document oriented database, and a shared key that increases query response time and offers a uniform data distribution in servers. The model can store huge amounts of data produced by RFID-IoT sensors and the system is efficiently utilized especially for supply chain management. The proposed model might need more work for some exceptional cases as mentioned by the author. An adaptive scheduling algorithm [18] had been proposed by Ghoneem & Kulkarni to reduce the execution time of Hadoop MapReduce in a heterogeneous and scalable environment. A classification algorithm is used to differentiate executable and non-executable jobs and process them accordingly. Issues like small job starvations are solved.

Smart City: Din et al. [12], the authors proposed architecture for smart cities using SDN enabled IoT-Big Data processing. Here, Hadoop clusters were used and modification to existing scheduling algorithm was done to adjust the computational load dynamically in a distributed environment. Thus, the given methodology helped to speed up the data pre-processing and analysis part further under resource constraint environment using the distributed computational environment. In the paper [19], authors Bi et al. proposed an IoT system based on SDN for smart city services. Experimentation was done to study time-constrained Big Data transfer scheduling problem. The proposed methodology helped in achieving lower transfer delay and improved network bandwidth utilization. This is accomplished by employing an SDN controller that allows dynamic flow control and scheduling the multi-flow transfer.

SDN-Based IoT for Big Data: The authors Kakiz et al. [20], proposed an SDN-based IoT architecture where sensor data are analyzed in the lower layer instead of the application layer to reduce traffic. It consists of four layers namely, perception, gateway, network (with a sub-layer called Controller Service) and application layer. OpenFlow gateways were used as gateways. Here each incoming packet received from the perception layer were evaluated to judge its usefulness.

If packets were found to be useful, it was sent to the upper layer and finally to the internet otherwise it is discarded, thus reducing the traffic on the Internet. An application-aware routing scheme for Big Data processing using SDN has been proposed by the authors Cheng and Wang in [21] to speed up the data shuffling over a network. They considered Hadoop Map Reduce for Big Data processing. The network topology employed is the Fat tree topology that is commonly used for scalability. SDN controllers receive the shuffling information from the Hadoop Controller and effectively allocate network resources. Results show that this scheme gives a better response than other similar schemes. The paper presents a Big Data network using SDN based IoT. The authors Xu et al. [22] states the problem associated a traditional network for Big Data transmission and how SDN can overcome them. The proposed architecture is flexible and meets the demands of Big Data transmission. As future work, they would like to implement the architecture with the simulation platform and improve SDN routing. Big Data transmission needs the support of the network. The authors Bedhief et al. in [23] presented a solution to overcome the heterogeneity of the network and IoT devices by adopting an SDN Docker-based architecture. SDN benefits like programmable configuration having a view of the overall network which helped to manage the heterogeneity of the network with docker. Thus it provides portability to the developers to create and deploy IoT applications easily.

In [24] Naik, the author of the paper, proposes a docker contained-based Big Data processing which is inexpensive and useful for everyone using multiple clouds.

Smart Grid: The authors Kaur et al. in [25], proposed a tensor-based Big Data management scheme for the dimensionality reduction of the data generated by smart devices in a Smart Grid System. SDN is used for minimizing the load and proper bandwidth utilization. In this scheme, data is represented in tensor form. Here Frobenius norm is applied to the high order tensors to reduce the reconstruction errors of the tensors. Next, an empirical probability based control scheme is designed to trace the best path for transferring the reduced data using SDN to achieve lower latency and higher QoS (quality of service).

Mobile Edge Computing: In the paper [26], the authors Wang et al. proposed an algorithm called Energy Efficient Sensor Selection and Routing (ESR), to reduce the energy consumption in SDN-IoT network where for Big Data processing Mobile Edge Computing (MEC) was applied. The algorithm comprises of three phases.

The overall energy consumption is reduced by cautiously finding optimal data reconstruction and aggregation, which is executed by SDN traffic engineering.

They have proved that ESR is a '$\alpha\ log|K|$' approximation algorithm, where K is the set of observed locations.

From the above, as discussed in the literature, it can be found that there are still major areas where further improvement needs to be done. Table 2 represents the proposed work and additional scope of improvement where the existing work can be further investigated.

4   Challenges and Issues Related to Big Data in SDN Based IoT

The extraction of meaningful data through Big Data analytic process in IoT is a challenge. This section provides some major challenges on this issue.

1. **Extraction:** There is a rapid generation of data as many IoT devices are connected to the Internet to provide accurate services. Not all data generated is useful that needs to be stored. These give rise to the problem for distinguishing between meaningful and redundant data. Therefore, proper mechanisms are required to filter only useful and meaningful data.
2. **Heterogeneous Data:** The heterogeneity of the IoT device producing data of different formats like text, voice, image, etc. needs to be handled. Noisy data need to be eliminated or corrected. Moreover, suitable data mining algorithms for each type of data need to be modified in order to deal with the IoT-Big Data.
3. **Storage:** Storage is another important concern in IoT-Big Data because the huge data need to be transmitted from the source to the server which eats up huge bandwidth as well as occupies large storage space. Data Redundancy is one of the biggest issues regarding storage [27]. Compressing the data and removing redundant data near the source will help to save both bandwidth and storage.
4. **Security:** The security of IoT devices has been an issue since long [28].
5. **Real-time Analysis:** Real-time analysis of the data from the sensors has become a mandate in most IoT environment. Achieving real-time response is little difficult because of the inherent network issues as well as the complexity of the data produced.
6. **Level of Analysis:** Another question of great concern to the Industry is the architectural level at which Big Data analysis should be done in the IoT environment.

5 Future Scope of Research

Although numerous problems related Big Data analysis of IoT in SDN based IoT were addressed by many other previous researchers, still there remains formidable amount of challenges in the area which needs further investigation for its efficient solutions. Some open research problems are presented below.

Table 2. Existing work with future scope.

Author	Proposed work	Future scope
Ding, G., Wang, L., Wu, Q. [13]	A practical approach to Big Data processing in IoT environment combatting issues like heterogeneity of data ,multidimensionality reduction of data etc.	More specific algorithms for IoT application purpose need to be investigated
Jabbar et al. [14]	Common form of computational tool for Big Data analytics using data fusion technique	Simpler and feasible query is needed for management of data and meta data. This is to be investigated out
Dinesh Kumar et al. [16]	Big Data analysis on health data using Hadoop and map reduce	Incorporating SDN based IoT will give an optimization of network utilization
Kang, Y. S. et al. [17]	Efficient data processing of RFID-IoT based data analysis using MongoDB	Enhancement needed for non-trivial query
Ghoneem and Kulkarni [18]	Adaptive scheduler for Hadoop Map Reduce Task	Sorting, searching on big clusters can be incorporated in the future as well as fairness in scheduling
Din et al. [12]	Architecture for smart cities using SDN enabled IoT-Big Data processing	More refined scheduling algorithm can be implemented to further reduce the Big Data processing
Bi et al. [19]	SDN architecture for smart cities to overcome time-constrained Big Data transfer scheduling	Support for different QoS requirement. Some lightweight action could be incorporated in the data layer
Kakiz et al. [20]	SDN-based IoT architecture using the lower layers for analysing the usefulness of data packets which needs to be retained thus reducing traffic at an early stage	Investigation on use of different types of SDN controllers those can be used to further strengthening the security of the system
Cheng et al. [21]	Application-aware routing scheme for Big Data processing using SDN	Different routing mechanisms need to be considered in delivering packets efficiently and achieving higher (QoS)
Xu et al. [22]	Big Data network using SDN based IoT	Implementation of the architecture with the simulation platform and improve SDN routing
Bedhief et al. [23]	SDN-docker based solution for heterogeneity of Big Data in IoT	The architecture has to be tested in different SDN controllers, which will be future work
Kaur et al. in [25]	Tensor-based Big Data management scheme for the dimensionality reduction of data in Smart Grid System	Implementation of this scheme in more systems
Wang et al. [26]	Algorithm for Energy Efficient Sensor Selection and Routing (ESR)	Practical implementation

1. Even if SDN controller helps in routing Big Data effectively in the IoT network, advanced protocols needs to be developed for the efficient utilization of network resources as well as their optimization and reliable operation.
2. Proper methodology for dimensionality reduction of the big IoT data has to be evolved out with lesser regeneration errors need to be investigated. Efforts should be given so that the developed methodology consumes lesser resources.
3. Further investigations are needed to facilitate SDN controllers to be able to control heterogeneous network more efficiently. Also methodology to be evolved so that

heterogeneity in smart devices and its developed heterogeneous data produced could be adequately handled.

4. Bringing down the computational requirement for resolving Big Data issues executable by the IoT devices, will help in improving the latency as well as bandwidth. This can be achieved through Edge computing or Fog computing which needs more further refinement in terms of further research investigation. Switches in SDN can be used as Fog nodes for the purpose. Efficient algorithm for the purpose could be investigated out.

5. **Level of Analysis:** Data generated from Infrastructure layer will be presented to the Application layer. There is a provision of data analysis at each of layer of the architecture. Development of efficient algorithm to work in both the layers for the purpose is also a challenge.

   (a) **Infrastructure Layer:** A low latency network performing Big Data analysis can be achieved in the Infrastructure layer. The data generated will be examined and processed within the same layer. Another advantage is that the required time for decision making in the upper layers will be greatly reduced based on this examined data.

   (b) **Network Layer:** The SDN-based network layer has controllers and switches which can be used for Big Data analysis as they are more powerful than the resource constrained devices in the Infrastructure layer for conventional IoT devices. Suitable Algorithms can be developed for the purpose using these resources which can resolve Big Data issues at shortest possible time.

   (c) **Application Layer:** In the application layer, Big Data analysis can be achieved using resources such as Hadoop, Apache Spark, Apache Storm, etc. running in the Cloud. These platforms can be accessed via APIs and the required data processing can be done there. These API's are light weighted and can be accessed from anywhere with proper authorization and authentication.

Investigations need to be carried out to develop suitable algorithms for resolving Big Data problem of IoT in the above mentioned architectural layers.

6. Since IoT system is a resource constrained system, research efforts are to made in the direction of developing lesser energy consumption methodology which will help optimal shuffle of Big Data in the network.

6   Conclusion

This paper discusses some past works related to Big Data issues generated by SDN based IoT architecture and how the previous workers tried to resolve this issue to facilitate Big Data analysis. Though this work has been initiated very recently so lot of research initiative are still pending to be resolved to be to give the SDN based IoT architecture a commercial shape. Some works have already been initiated which are discussed here as review model. Various potential challenges are also discussed in this paper which needed to be resolved to have smooth processing of the Big Data in IoT environment. Some key research works in the area of Big Data analysis in IoT have been presented in this paper. SDN structure of IoT plays a key role in IoT based Big Data analysis endeavour. This solution was possible due to the dynamic behaviour of the SDN controllers.

References

1. Ahmed, E., Yaqoob, I., Gani, A., Imran, M., Guizani, M.: Internet-of-Things-based smart environments: state of the art, taxonomy, and open research challenges. IEEE Wirel. Commun. **23**(5), 10–16 (2016). https://doi.org/10.1109/MWC.2016.7721736
2. Cisco Visual Networking Index: Forecast and Trends. http://www.cisco.com/c/en/us/soluti ons/collateral/service-provider/visual-networking-index-vni/white-paper-c11-741490.html. Accessed 15 Dec 2018
3. Cai, H., Xu, B., Jiang, L., Vasilakos, A.V.: IoT-based big data storage systems in cloud computing: perspectives and challenges. IEEE Internet of Things J. **4**(1), 75–87 (2017). https:// doi.org/10.1109/JIOT.2016.2619369
4. Das, R.K., Maji, A.K., Saha, G.: Prospect of improving internet of things by incorporating software-defined network. In: Bera, R., Sarkar, S., Singh, O., Saikia, H. (eds.) Advances in Communication, Devices and Networking. Lecture Notes in Electrical Engineering, vol. 537, pp. 537–544. Springer, Singapore (2019). https://doi.org/10.1007/978-981-13-3450-4_58
5. Alqarni, M.A.: Benefits of SDN for big data applications. In: 2017 14th International Conference on Smart Cities: Improving Quality of Life Using ICT & IoT (HONET-ICT), pp. 74–77. IEEE (2017). https://doi.org/10.1109/honet.2017.8102206
6. Cui, L., Yu, F.R., Yan, Q.: When big data meets software-defined networking: SDN for big data and big data for SDN. IEEE Network **30**(1), 58–65 (2016). https://doi.org/10.1109/MNET. 2016.7389832
7. Gudivada, V.N., Baeza-Yates, R., Raghavan, V.V.: Big data: promises and problems. Computer **3**, 20–23 (2015). https://doi.org/10.1109/MC.2015.62
8. Zhang, J., Yao, X., Han, G., Gui, Y.: A survey of recent technologies and challenges in big data utilization. In: 2015 International Conference on Information and Communication Technology Convergence (ICTC), pp. 497–499. IEEE (2015). https://doi.org/10.1109/ictc. 2015.7354594
9. Yetis, Y., Sara, R.G., Erol, B.A., Kaplan, H., Akuzum, A., Jamshidi, M.: Application of big data analytics via cloud computing. In: World Automation Congress (WAC), pp. 1–5. IEEE (2016). https://doi.org/10.1109/wac.2016.7582986
10. Hadoop. https://searchdatamanagement.techtarget.com/definition/Hadoop. Last accessed 15 Dec 2018
11. Marjani, M., et al.: Big IoT data analytics: architecture, opportunities, and open research challenges. IEEE Access **5**, 5247–5261 (2017). https://doi.org/10.1109/ACCESS.2017.268 9040
12. Din, S., Rathore, M.M., Ahmad, A., Paul, A., Khan, M.: SDIoT: software defined internet of thing to analyze big data in smart cities. In: 2017 IEEE 42nd Conference on Local Computer Networks Workshops (LCN Workshops), pp. 175–182. IEEE (2017). https://doi.org/10.1109/ lcn.workshops.2017.84
13. Ding, G., Wang, L., & Wu, Q.: Big Data analytics in future Internet of Things. The computing research repository (CoRR), pp. 1–6. arXiv preprint arXiv:1311.4112 (2013)
14. Jabbar, S., et al.: A methodology of real-time data fusion for localized big data analytics. IEEE Access **6**, 24510–24520 (2018). https://doi.org/10.1109/ACCESS.2018.2820176
15. Alam, F., Mehmood, R., Katib, I., Albeshri, A.: Analysis of eight data mining algorithms for smarter Internet of Things (IoT). Procedia Comput. Sci. **98**, 437–442 (2016). https://doi.org/ 10.1016/j.procs.2016.09.068. Elsevier

16. Dineshkumar, P., SenthilKumar, R., Sujatha, K., Ponmagal, R.S., Rajavarman, V.N.: Big data analytics of IoT based health care monitoring system. In: IEEE International Conference on Electrical, Computer and Electronics Engineering (UPCON), pp. 55–60. IEEE (2016). https://doi.org/10.1109/upcon.2016.7894624

17. Kang, Y.S., Park, I.H., Rhee, J., Lee, Y.H.: MongoDB-based repository design for IoT-generated RFID/sensor big data. IEEE Sens. J. **16**(2), 485–497 (2016). https://doi.org/10.1109/JSEN.2015.2483499

18. Mohammad, G., Lalit, K.: An adaptive mapreduce scheduler for scalable heterogeneous systems. In: Satapathy, S., Bhateja, V., Joshi, A. (eds.) Proceedings of the International Conference on Data Engineering and Communication Technology. Advances in Intelligent Systems and Computing, vol 469. Springer, Singapore (2017). https://doi.org/10.1007/978-981-10-1678-3_57

19. Bi, Y., Lin, C., Zhou, H., Yang, P., Shen, X., Zhao, H.: Time-constrained big data transfer for SDN-enabled smart city. IEEE Commun. Mag. **55**(12), 44–50 (2017). https://doi.org/10.1109/MCOM.2017.1700236

20. Kakiz, M.T., Öztürk, E., Çavdar, T.: A novel SDN-based IoT architecture for big data. In: 2017 International Conference on Artificial Intelligence and Data Processing Symposium (IDAP), pp. 1–5. IEEE (2017). https://doi.org/10.1109/idap.2017.8090186

21. Cheng, L.W., Wang, S.Y.: Application-aware SDN routing for big data networking. In: Global Communications Conference (GLOBECOM), pp. 1–6. IEEE (2015). https://doi.org/10.1109/glocom.2015.7417577

22. Xu, Y., Sun, Z., Sun, Z.: SDN-based architecture for big data network. In: 2017 International Conference on Cyber-Enabled Distributed Computing and Knowledge Discovery (CyberC), pp. 513–516. IEEE (2017). https://doi.org/10.1109/cyberc.2017

23. Bedhief, I., Kassar, M., Aguili, T.: SDN-based Architecture challenging the IoT heterogeneity. In: Smart Cloud Networks & Systems (SCNS), pp. 1–3. IEEE (2016). https://doi.org/10.1109/scns.2016.7870558

24. Naik, N.: Docker container-based big data processing system in multiple clouds for everyone. In: Systems Engineering Symposium (ISSE), pp. 1–7. IEEE (2017). https://doi.org/10.1109/syseng.2017.8088294

25. Kaur, D., Aujla, G.S., Kumar, N., Zomaya, A., Ranjan, R.: Tensor-based big data management scheme for dimensionality reduction problem in smart grid systems: SDN perspective. IEEE Trans. Knowl. Data Eng. **30**(10), 1985–1998 (2018). https://doi.org/10.1109/TKDE.2018.2809747

26. Wang, C.H., Kuo, J.J., Yang, D.N., Chen, W.T.: Green software-defined internet of things for big data processing in mobile edge networks. In: 2018 IEEE International Conference on Communications (ICC), pp. 1–7. IEEE (2018). https://doi.org/10.1109/ICC.2018.8422236

27. RubyDinakar, J., Vagdevi, S.: A Study on storage mechanism for heterogeneous sensor data on big data paradigm. In: International Conference on Electrical, Electronics, Communication, Computer, and Optimization Techniques (ICEECCOT), pp. 342–345. IEEE (2017). https://doi.org/10.1109/iceeccot.2017.8284525

28. Sezer, O.B., Dogdu, E., Ozbayoglu, A.M.: Context-aware computing, learning, and big data in internet of things: a survey. IEEE Internet Things J. **5**(1), 1–27 (2018). https://doi.org/10.1109/JIOT.2017.2773600

Classification of Diffuse Lung Diseases Using Heterogeneous Ensemble Classifiers

Shyla Raj[1]([⊠]) [iD], D. S. Vinod[1] [iD], and Nagaraj Murthy[2] [iD]

[1] Department of Information Science and Engineering, Sri Jayachamarajendra College of Engineering, Mysuru, Karnataka, India
shylanataraj@gmail.com, dsvinod@daad-alumni.de
[2] Department of Radiology, JSS Medical College, Mysuru, Karnataka, India
nagnishu@gmail.com

Abstract. Accurate classification of Diffuse Lung Diseases (DLD) plays a significant role in the identification of the lung pathology. Efficient classifiers based on various learning strategies have been proposed for multi class DLD classification. Due to imbalance in DLD class distribution the mis-classification probability of minority class is higher when compared to the majority class. To overcome the affects of imbalance in class distribution, the sampling approach is employed in the work, to balance the training set. It is observed that recognition rate of each DLD class is distinct based on the learning method adopted. Thus the complementary information offered by each classifier can be fused effectively to boost the classification performance. A heterogeneous ensemble classifier method based on weighted majority voting scheme is presented in this work to classify five DLD patterns imaged in High Resolution Computed Tomography (HRCT). The efficiency of the base and ensemble classifier is assessed based on recall, precision, F-measure and G-mean measure. By comparison it is found the results by ensemble of classifiers is superior than compared to its base classifiers.

Keywords: Diffuse lung diseases · Voting · Ensemble · TALISMAN · Classification

1 Introduction

DLDs are the diverse group of irreversible pulmonary disorders which causes difficulty in breathing and if untreated results in death. Globally the death rate due to DLD has increased by about 6% in the last decade [29]. Since the symptoms exhibited by DLDs are similar, the HRCT scans are utilized for accurate diagnosis. The HRCT modality is chosen because it shows significant difference between healthy and affected lung tissues. But manually investigating HRCT is strenuous due to inter and intra class variations among the lung patterns and subjective errors that may arise due to inexperience of the radiologist. Thus research has been ongoing to build Computer-Aided Diagnosis (CAD) to support the radiologist in the interpretation of HRCT scans. Identification/classification of lung patterns is one of the most step in CAD system.

© Springer Nature Switzerland AG 2020
R. Patgiri et al. (Eds.): BigDML 2019, CCIS 1317, pp. 83–94, 2020.
https://doi.org/10.1007/978-3-030-62625-9_8

During the conduction of applied research Hansen and Salamon [21] discovered that the prediction made by combination of classifiers achieve better classification results than compared to its individual counterparts. This observation has motivated this work to use ensemble of classifiers to classify DLD patterns. Ensemble learning is a machine learning framework in which individual decision of set of classifiers are fused in a particular way to achieve better classification. The decisions of three heterogeneous classifiers viz. Gaussian Support Vector Machine (GSVM), Weighted k Nearest Neighbour (Wk-NN) and Decision Tree (DT) are combined using weighted majority voting scheme in the work. The work focuses on classification of five DLD patterns namely: Emphysema (E), Fibrosis (F), Ground Glass Opacity (GGO), Healthy (H) and Micro-Nodules (MN).

Alike the other medical classification problems, the DLDs also suffers from the imbalance in the class distribution. The rate of occurrence of each pathology is distinct and hence some classes has fewer instances than the other. Applying classification on such dataset results in false assessment of overall accuracy. Since most of the machine learning algorithm aims to achieve higher overall accuracy, it tries to over-fit the majority class and neglect the minority class. This adversely affects the recognition rate of minority class. To overcome this problem, the minority class in the training set is oversampled in feature space to match the majority class. The Synthetic Minority Oversampling Technique (SMOTE) algorithm [7] is used for generating the synthetic samples.

To our best knowledge, this is the first work to address the imbalance in class distribution of'TALISMAN' dataset by using the oversampling technique and adopt voting technique in ensemble learning for DLD pattern classification.

2   Related Work

Classification of DLDs is an important step in the CAD system for developed for differential diagnosis of DLD. The commonly used classifier include the Bayesian classifier, k-NN classifier, random forest and the widely utilized classifier in the literature is SVM. The works [36] and [6] employ the bayesian classifier, the k-NN classifier is used in [12, 26, 32]. The SVM is applied in [1, 3, 24, 25] and [14]. The feed forward neural network is adopted in [15, 16] and back propagation neural network in [35]. By analysing the above classification results it is observed that wrongly classified samples by each of the distinct classifiers is usually different. The DLD class wise recognition varies based on the learning technique employed in the classifier. Thus effective fusion of the complementary information from each classifiers can be used to boost the efficiency of DLD classification system. The multi-classifier approach or the ensemble learning is widely used in literature for various pattern recognition problems.

Dash et al. [10] presented a multi-classifier approach on the basis of winning neuron strategy for lung tissue classification. The work used the results of Neural Network (NN) and Naive Bayesian (NB) classifiers. Onan et al. [31] has employed ensemble classifier for text sentiment analysis. The decisions of NB, SVM, Logistic Regression, Discriminant Analysis and Bayesian Logistic Regression are fused using weighted voting scheme. Ye et al. [38] presented a decision machine based on weighted majority voting. The machine combined the benefits of SVM and Artificial Neural Network (ANN) for fault diagnosis. The network traffic was classified using multi classification approach in [9]. The method explored combination techniques such as majority voting, weighted majority voting, Naive Bayes, Dempster-Shafer combiner, Behavior-Knowledge Space (BKS), Wernecke's (WER) method and oracle. Bashir et al. [4] proposed a novel ensemble learning based on enhanced bagging technique for heart diseases prediction. The framework was built using NB, quadratic discriminant analysis, SVM, linear regression and instance based learner.

3 Dataset

The work uses benchmark 'TALISMAN' dataset [13]. A total of 11, 053 patches of size 32×32 are extracted from the provided 1946 2-D Annotated Region Of Interest (AROI). The pattern wise distribution of DLD patches is represented in the Table 1. It can be inferred from Table 1 that the dataset is skewed in distribution.

Table 1. The DLD pattern wise distribution selected for work

DLD type	E	F	GGO	H	MN
Total samples	422	2989	2226	3032	2384

4 Methodology

The Algorithm 1 explains the steps of classifier ensemble employed in the work. In the first step, texture features are extracted for the entire dataset using Fuzzy Local Binary Pattern (FLBP), Grey Level Occurrence Matrix (GLCM) and Grey level Run length Matrix (GLRLM) and Intensity feature from Intensity Histogram (IH). In the second step, the dataset is divided into training and testing set by using stratified partitioning technique. The third step involves generating the synthetic samples for training set in feature space by oversampling using SMOTE algorithm. The fourth step involves classification. The GSVM, Wk-NN and DT are used as base classifier. In the final step, individual decisions from the base classifiers are fused by using weighted majority voting scheme to get the final class labels.

4.1 Feature Extraction

The DLD patterns are manifested as textural alternation in lung parenchyma hence texture based features are extracted in the work.

Algorithm 1: Ensemble classification

Data: The DLD image patches p=$\{p_1, p_2, \ldots, p_n\}$

Result: Final class labels of DLD patches $X' = \{X_1', X_2', \ldots, X_N'\}$

Step 1: Compute Texture and Intensity features for all DLD patches
$Feature\_Vector = \{$FLBP; GLRLM; GLCM;IH$\}$

Step 2: Generate training and testing sets by using stratified
partitioning technique.

Step 3: Balance the training set using SMOTE in feature space

Step 4: Train GSVM, WK-NN and DT classifiers in parallel

Step 5: Obtain class labels for test data individually from trained
classifiers $X^1 = \{X_1^1, X_2^1, \ldots, X_N^1\}$; $X^2 = \{X_1^2, X_2^2, \ldots, X_N^2\}$;
$X^3 = \{X_1^3, X_2^3, \ldots, X_N^3\}$

Step 6: Determine final class label of test data X' by performing
$weighted\_majority\_voting = (X^1; X^2; X^3)$ (calls Algorithm 2)

FLBP proposed by Naresh and Nagendraswamy [30] is used in the work. FLBP is a powerful textural descriptor which overcomes the disadvantage of hard thresholding of the traditional LBP approach. The intensity of the image is transformed according to fuzzy triangular membership. Further the difference between center pixel and the neighbourhood is calculated and histogram is created. The main advantage of FLBP is that it gives both spatial and statistical information. For the work, FLBP patterns with 10 bins is extracted.

GLCM is a 2nd order statistical method proposed by Haralick et al. [22]. GLCM can be used to analyse the spatial distribution of pixel intensities. GLCM yields a 2-D matrix which gives information about how frequently pixel with intensity 'a' appear in particular spatial relationship with pixel with intensity 'b'. The spatial relationship between pixels in analysed by considering the neighbouring properties of the 26-connected neighbours. From each orientation nine features are calculated. Finally corresponding values in all orientations are averaged to obtain final resultant vector. Nine GLCM features are used in the work [37].

GLRLM is also a 2nd order statistical method proposed by Galloway [18] which yields a 2-D matrix RLM(a, b) which defines the relation between number of runs of gray level 'a' of length 'b' in a particular orientation. This matrix represents information regarding the connected length of a particular pixel in a particular direction. Run lengths are acquired in thirteen directions. In each direction the thirteen texture features [37] are acquired from the RLM matrix. The final GLRLM vector is calculated by averaging each of GLRLM feature in all directions.

4.2 Addressing Class Imbalance

In the medical recognition problems the recognition of each class is crucial, applying classification on dataset with imbalanced class distribution results in false assessment of overall accuracy because classifiers in general are biased towards the majority class and tend to neglect the minority class. Hence the imbalance in class distribution need to be addressed. In the work, the oversampling approach is applied to balance only the training dataset and imbalance in testing set prevails.

The SMOTE algorithm, is an oversampling technique which creates synthetic samples in feature space for minority class from the existing minority samples instead of simply creating their copies. The SMOTE finds the n-nearest neighbours for each sample in minority class and takes the difference between the neighbours. The difference is multiplied with a random number between 0 and 1. This value generates a new point i.e. sample between the existing neighbours. The class re-distribution of DLD patches after employing SMOTE is represented in Table 2 respectively.

Table 2. The DLD pattern wise distribution after sampling

DLD type	E	F	GGO	H	MN
Training set	2124	2092	2118	2122	2119
Testing set	127	897	668	910	715

4.3 Classification

According to Krogh and Vedelsby [27] to built a good ensemble classifiers, the base classifiers must be accurate and as diverse as possible. The diversity of classifier refers to the learning approach adopted or in sub sampling the training examples. The SVM belongs to the family of generalized linear classifiers while k-NN belongs to the family of instance-based learning and the DT constructs tree like structure to classify the data. Thus three diverse classifiers GSVM, Wk-NN and DT are chosen for the work.

SVM. The SVM with the Gaussian kernel [2] is used for categorization of the DLD patterns. The one-versus-one (OVO) strategy is used for multi-class categorization. In the OVO approach a separate classifier is trained for each pair of class label. Thus it involves $M(M - 1)/2$ classifier for M class problem. All $M(M - 1)/2$ classifiers are involved in predicting the class label of unlabelled sample and sample is given the class label for which it gets majority number of votes. The best values of regularization parameter 'C' and the kernel width σ is found using trial and error approach on the training set.

Wk-NN. The Wk-NN a variation of traditional K-nn is used in the work [5]. The Wk-nn overcomes the shortcoming of simple majority voting employed in k-nn. In the Wk-nn each neighbour $n_i \epsilon ne_K(x)$ is associated with a weight w_n, where $ne_K(x) = \{n_1, n_2, \ldots, n_K\}$ are K points selected from training data. For each test data point to be classified different set of weights are assigned to the neighbour based on its inverse distance from new data point i.e. the neighbours closer to the test data point will have a greater influence than neighbours that are further away. This method gives more importance or greater weightage to the neighbours that are close to the test data point and the decision is less affected by the neighbours that are far from the new data point.

Decision Tree. Decision tree is a supervised, non-parametric learning algorithm [17]. The decision tree learns decision rules from labelled training data by constructing tree structure in the form of flowchart. The internal node of the tree presents the test on the attribute, every branch depicts the result of the test and every leaf node represents the class label. The decision tree can be easily transformed into if-then-else classification rules. Given a testing data, for which class is unknown, the target class is estimated by testing the data against the constructed decision tree.

4.4 Voting Scheme

Voting techniques are simple, efficient and widely used method for decision fusion. The voting technique can be weighted or un-weighted. In un-weighted/simple majority voting scheme the final decision X' is the output which atleast more than half number of base classifiers C agree on.

$$X' = mode\{C_1(y), C_2(y) \ldots C_n(y)\} \tag{1}$$

In weighted majority scheme [8] each base classifier is assigned with the weights. The weights to the classifier are assigned automatically based on the misclassification cost (ϵ_i) [38]. The weight (w_i) is inversely proportional to the misclassification cost, mathematically it is writtenas:

$$w_i = log_2((1 - \epsilon_i)/\epsilon_i) \tag{2}$$

The individual weights are normalized such that sum of all weights equals to 1. The final decision X' is the one for which summation of individual classifier decision with its corresponding weights, is the highest. The final decision X' of weighted majority is given as follows:

$$X' = argmax_j \sum_{i=1}^{N} w_i \chi L(C_i(y) = j) \tag{3}$$

where L is the set of unique class labels and χL is the characteristic function:

$$\left[C_i(y) = j \epsilon L \right] \tag{4}$$

Algorithm 2 explains the weighted majority voting scheme.

Algorithm 2: Weighted majority voting

Data: Class label of individual classifier $X^1 = \{X_1^1, X_2^1, \ldots, X_N^1\}$; $X^2 = \{X_1^2, X_2^2, \ldots, X_N^2\}$; $X^3 = \{X_1^3, X_2^3, \ldots, X_N^3\}$
  Weights for individual classifier w= $\{w_1, w_2, w_3\}$

Result: Final class label $X' = \{X_1', X_2', \ldots, X_N'\}$

Step 1: Gather the class label from individual classifier.

Step 2: Calculate the weights of individual classifier using equation (2).

Step 3: Final class label is deduced by considering the majority of the individual weighted decision as shown in equation (3).

4.5   Experimental Set-up and Evaluation Metric

A stratified ten cross fold validation technique is used to evaluate the efficiency of the ensemble classifier. The stratification approach is employed on both balanced and imbalanced dataset, to ensure that representative samples from each class should appear in both training and testing set. The simple majority voting scheme assigns equal weights to all the classifier whereas in the weighted majority voting scheme the weights to the classifiers are assigned based on the performance of the classifier.

The classification performance is evaluated on the basis of Recall, Precision, Fscore and G-mean measures. In the medical research domain, the main goal is to reduce the false negatives. Hence to gauge the efficiency of ensemble classification, recall measure is used. The precision measure is equally important as recall as it defines the classifier's exactness. A high precision value indicates lower number of False Positives. F-score is a weighted average measured based precision and recall value. G-mean is the harmonic mean of sensitivity and specificity which provides better assessment of classifier than the accuracy measure in case of imbalanced dataset.

5   Result and Discussion

Table 3 shows the performance comparison between the individual base classifiers and the results obtained from the voting scheme for imbalanced dataset. Amongst the voting schemes it can be noted that the performance of the simple majority performs better in terms of recall and G-mean than the weighted majority but it fails in achieving higher Precision. Hence weighted majority voting is considered better than simple voting.

Table 3. Performance comparison of base classifiers and ensemble classifier for imbalanced dataset

Method	GSVM	WKNN	DT	Simple majority	Weighted majority
Recall	69.12	74.12	73.16	78.16	76.54
Precision	84.14	76.50	77.24	82.35	85.16
F-score	71.26	75.25	74.59	79.78	79.24
G-mean	78.39	83.49	82.58	86.03	84.84

Table 4 gives more insights about how different classes of DLDs are recognised by each learning algorithm. As mentioned earlier each individual classifier identifies DLD type distinctly based on the learning technique adopted. The Emphysema (E) and Micro-nodules (MN) is well recognized by WKNN while Fibrosis (F), Healthy (H) and Ground Glass Opacity (GGO) by GSVM. It can be noted that, no individual classifier is able to recognize all lung patterns effectively. Thus fusing the individual decisions helps in the overall performance improvement of multi-class classification problem.

It can be noticed from Table 4 that the recall measures of minority class E, GGO and MN are lower than the rest in imbalanced dataset. This is because, the classifier

Table 4. Illustration of recall measure of each DLD class for imbalanced dataset

Method	GSVM	WKNN	DT	Weighted majority
Emphysema (E)	19.61	57.87	49.08	48.03
Fibrosis (F)	93.86	81.85	85.16	91.39
Ground Glass Opacity (GGO)	74.51	74.03	73.83	78.10
Healthy (H)	85.35	81.12	83.12	87.08
Micro-nodules (MN)	76.28	76.85	74.96	78.08

tries to improve the recognition rate of the majority class while the mis-classification of minority class is neglected. To overcome this bias, oversampling the minority class is employed to match them to majority class.

Table 5 depicts the performance comparison between the individual base classifiers and the results obtained from ensemble classifier. These results are obtained after balancing the dataset. In here the weighted majority voting performs better than the simple majority voting in all measures. On comparing the results of ensemble with base classifiers, it can be noted that there is considerable improvement in results by the ensemble classifier.

Table 5. Performance comparison of base classifiers and ensemble classifier for balanced data

Method	GSVM	WKNN	DT	Simple majority	Weighted majority
Recall	76.38	76.36	75.49	79.95	80.24
Precision	81.79	74.13	71.10	80.54	81.23
F-score	78.28	75.03	72.18	80.14	80.62
G-mean	84.73	84.78	84.23	87.20	87.40

The class wise recall value obtained for balanced dataset is presented in Table 6. It can be well noted that the recognition of the minority class patterns E, GGO and MN has been enhanced after re-balancing the dataset. Contrasting the results between balanced Table 6 and imbalanced data Table 4, it can be perceived that balancing the dataset helps in the recognition of all DLD types, thus improving the overall recognition performance.

Table 7 illustrates the comparison result of proposed ensemble classifier with existing work in literature. By contrasting the results, it can be inferred that proposed method provides promising results than the most of existing work.

The results of class-wise recall comparison of proposed work with other state of art techniques in literature is tabulated in Table 8. The recognition rate for the Fibrosis (F) pattern by the proposed method outperforms all the existing methods including deep learning [19]. The recognition rate of Ground Glass (GGO) and Healthy (H) are equally promising when compared to other existing methods. While Emphysema (E) and Micronodules (Mn) patterns need further analysis to improve their recognition.

Table 6. Illustration of recall measure of each DLD class for balanced dataset

Method	GSVM	WKNN	DT	Weighted majority
Emphysema (E)	55.91	71.50	70.24	69.61
Fibrosis (F)	92.80	80.56	79.98	89.31
Ground Glass Opacity (GGO)	77.56	75.30	78.29	80.66
Healthy (H)	83.10	77.71	75.37	84.13
Micro-nodules (MN)	72.53	76.74	73.58	77.50

Table 7. Contrasting the proposed work with existing work in literature

Method	Recall (%)	Precision (%)	F-score (%)
Proposed	80.2	81.2	80.6
Joyseeree et al. (2018) [24]	74.5	80.7	77.1
Song et al. (2015) [33]	84.1	82.5	83.3
Song et al. (2013) [34]	82.6	80.7	81.5
Li et al. (2013) [28]	74.4	70.2	na
Depeursinge et al. (2012) [14]	75.8	76.3	76

Table 8. The DLD pattern wise comparison of proposed work with existing work in literature

Method	E (%)	F (%)	GGO (%)	H (%)	Mn (%)
Proposed	69.61	89.31	80.66	84.13	77.50
Joyseeree et al. (2018) [24]	57.25	82.41	72.73	72.6	87.54
Gao et al. (2016) [19]	82.70	89.10	81.51	91.42	87.99
Gupta et al. (2016) [20]	75.00	71.8	62.00	81.20	71.4
Shin et al. (2016) [23]	91.0	83.0	70.0	68.0	79.0
Song et al. (2015) [33]	79.6	85.4	80	88.5	87.2
Depeursinge et al. (2012) [11]	72.70	84.20	68.40	82.70	83.50

6 Conclusion

The oversampling approach has been adopted in the work to overcome the imbalance in the class distribution and the bias towards minority class. An ensemble classifier based on weighted majority voting is presented for multi-class categorization of DLD patterns. The individual decisions of the base classifiers are fused to achieve higher classification efficiency. The experimental results clear exhibit the performance boost in Recall, Precision, F-score and G-mean values by ensemble classifier than its base classifier. Thus it can be concluded that balancing the dataset and adopting ensemble approach for classification helps in improving the overall performance of multi-class DLD classification problem.

References

1. Ajin, M., Mredhula, L.: Diagnosis of interstitial lung disease by pattern classification. Procedia Comput. Sci. **115**, 195–208 (2017)
2. Amari, S.I., Wu, S.: Improving support vector machine classifiers by modifying kernel functions. Neural Netw. **12**(6), 783–789 (1999)
3. Bagesteiro, L.D., Oliveira, L.F., Weingaertner, D.: Blockwise classification of lung patterns in unsegmented CT images. In: 2015 IEEE 28th International Symposium on Computer-Based Medical Systems (CBMS), pp. 177–182. IEEE (2015)
4. Bashir, S., Qamar, U., Khan, F.H.: BagMOOV: a novel ensemble for heart disease prediction bootstrap aggregation with multi-objective optimized voting. Aust. Phys. Eng. Sci. Med. **38**(2), 305–323 (2015)
5. Bicego, M., Loog, M.: Weighted k-nearest neighbor revisited. In: 2016 23rd International Conference on Pattern Recognition (ICPR), pp. 1642–1647. IEEE (2016)
6. Chabat, F., Yang, G.Z., Hansell, D.M.: Obstructive lung diseases: texture classification for differentiation at ct. Radiology **228**(3), 871–877 (2003)
7. Chawla, N.V., Bowyer, K.W., Hall, L.O., Kegelmeyer, W.P.: SMOTE: synthetic minority over-sampling technique. J. Artif. Intell. Res. **16**, 321–357 (2002)
8. Cordella, Luigi P., De Stefano, C., Fontanella, F., Scotto di Freca, A.: A weighted majority vote strategy using Bayesian Networks. In: Petrosino, A. (ed.) ICIAP 2013. LNCS, vol. 8157, pp. 219–228. Springer, Heidelberg (2013). https://doi.org/10.1007/978-3-642-41184-7_23
9. Dainotti, A., Pescapé, A., Sansone, C.: Early classification of network traffic through multi-classification. In: Domingo-Pascual, J., Shavitt, Y., Uhlig, S. (eds.) TMA 2011. LNCS, vol. 6613, pp. 122–135. Springer, Heidelberg (2011). https://doi.org/10.1007/978-3-642-20305-3_11
10. Dash, J.K., Mukhopadhyay, S., Garg, M.K., Prabhakar, N., Khandelwal, N.: Multiclassifier framework for lung tissue classification. In: Students' Technology Symposium (TechSym), 2014 IEEE, pp. 264–269. IEEE (2014)
11. Depeursinge, A., Foncubierta–Rodriguez, A., Van de Ville, D., Müller, H.: Multiscale lung texture signature learning using the Riesz transform. In: Ayache, N., Delingette, H., Golland, P., Mori, K. (eds.) MICCAI 2012. LNCS, vol. 7512, pp. 517–524. Springer, Heidelberg (2012). https://doi.org/10.1007/978-3-642-33454-2_64
12. Depeursinge, A., Sage, D., Hidki, A., Platon, A., Poletti, P.A., Unser, M., Muller, H.: Lung tissue classification using wavelet frames. In: 2007 29th Annual International Conference of the IEEE Engineering in Medicine and Biology Society, EMBS 2007, pp. 6259–6262. IEEE (2007)
13. Depeursinge, A., Vargas, A., Platon, A., Geissbuhler, A., Poletti, P.A., Müller, H.: Building a reference multimedia database for interstitial lung diseases. Comput. Med. Imaging Graph. **36**(3), 227–238 (2012)
14. Depeursinge, A., Van de Ville, D., Platon, A., Geissbuhler, A., Poletti, P.A., Muller, H.: Near-affine-invariant texture learning for lung tissue analysis using isotropic wavelet frames. IEEE Trans. Inf Technol. Biomed. **16**(4), 665–675 (2012)
15. Dudhane, A., Shingadkar, G., Sanghavi, P., Jankharia, B., Talbar, S.: Interstitial lung disease classification using feed forward neural networks. In: ICCASP, Advances in Intelligent Systems Research, vol. 137, pp. 515–521 (2017)

16. Dudhane, Akshay A., Talbar, Sanjay N.: Multi-scale directional mask pattern for medical image classification and retrieval. In: Chaudhuri, Bidyut B., Kankanhalli, Mohan S., Raman, B. (eds.) Proceedings of 2nd International Conference on Computer Vision & Image Processing. AISC, vol. 703, pp. 345–357. Springer, Singapore (2018). https://doi.org/10.1007/978-981-10-7895-8_27

17. Friedl, M.A., Brodley, C.E.: Decision tree classification of land cover from remotely sensed data. Remote Sens. Environ. **61**(3), 399–409 (1997)

18. Galloway, M.M.: Texture analysis using grey level run lengths. NASA STI/Recon Technical Report N 75 (1974)

19. Gao, M., et al.: Holistic classification of ct attenuation patterns for interstitial lung diseases via deep convolutional neural networks. Comput. Methods in Biomech. Biomed. Eng. Imaging Vis. **6**(1), 1–6 (2018)

20. Gupta, R.D., Dash, J.K., Mukhopadhyay, S.: Content based retrieval of interstitial lung disease patterns using spatial distribution of intensity, gradient magnitude and gradient direction. In: 2016 International Conference on Systems in Medicine and Biology (ICSMB), pp. 58–61. IEEE (2016)

21. Hansen, L.K., Salamon, P.: Neural network ensembles. IEEE Trans. Pattern Anal. Mach. Intell. **12**(10), 993–1001 (1990)

22. Haralick, R.M., Shanmugam, K., et al.: Textural features for image classification. IEEE Trans. Syst. Man Cybern. **6**, 610–621 (1973)

23. Hoo-Chang, S., et al.: Deep convolutional neural networks for computer-aided detection: CNN architectures, dataset characteristics and transfer learning. IEEE Trans. Med. Imaging **35**(5), 1285 (2016)

24. Joyseeree, R., Müller, H., Depeursinge, A.: Rotation-covariant tissue analysis for interstitial lung diseases using learned steerable filters: performance evaluation and relevance for diagnostic aid. Comput. Med. Imaging Graph. **64**, 1–11 (2018)

25. Kale, M., Mukhopadhyay, S., Dash, J.K., Garg, M., Khandelwal, N.: Differentiation of several interstitial lung disease patterns in HRCT images using support vector machine: role of databases on performance. In: Medical Imaging 2016: Computer-Aided Diagnosis, vol. 9785, p. 97852Z. International Society for Optics and Photonics (2016)

26. Korfiatis, P.D., Karahaliou, A.N., Kazantzi, A.D., Kalogeropoulou, C., Costaridou, L.I.: Texture-based identification and characterization of interstitial pneumonia patterns in lung multidetector CT. IEEE Trans. Inf Technol. Biomed. **14**(3), 675–680 (2010)

27. Krogh, A., Vedelsby, J.: Neural network ensembles, cross validation, and active learning. In: Advances in Neural Information Processing Systems, pp. 231–238 (1995)

28. Li, Q., Cai, W., Feng, D.D.: Lung image patch classification with automatic feature learning. In: 2013 35th Annual International Conference of the IEEE Engineering in Medicine and Biology Society (EMBC), pp. 6079–6082. IEEE (2013)

29. Naghavi, M., et al.: Global, regional, and national age-sex specific mortality for 264 causes of death, 1980–2016: a systematic analysis for the global burden of disease study 2016. Lancet **390**(10100), 1151–1210 (2017)

30. Naresh, Y., Nagendraswamy, H.: A novel fuzzy LBP based symbolic representation technique for classification of medicinal plants. In: 2015 3rd IAPR Asian Conference on Pattern Recognition (ACPR), pp. 524–528. IEEE (2015)

31. Onan, A., Korukoğlu, S., Bulut, H.: A multiobjective weighted voting ensemble classifier based on differential evolution algorithm for text sentiment classification. Expert Syst. Appl. **62**, 1–16 (2016)

32. Sluimer, I.C., van Waes, P.F., Viergever, M.A., van Ginneken, B.: Computer-aided diagnosis in high resolution ct of the lungs. Med. Phys. **30**(12), 3081–3090 (2003)

33. Song, Y., Cai, W., Huang, H., Zhou, Y., Wang, Y., Feng, D.D.: Locality-constrained subcluster representation ensemble for lung image classification. Med. Image Anal. **22**(1), 102–113 (2015)

34. Song, Y., Cai, W., Zhou, Y., Feng, D.D.: Feature-based image patch approximation for lung tissue classification. IEEE Trans. Med. Imaging **32**(4), 797–808 (2013)

35. Uchiyama, Y., et al.: Quantitative computerized analysis of diffuse lung disease in high-resolution computed tomography. Med. Phys. **30**(9), 2440–2454 (2003)

36. Uppaluri, R., Hoffman, E.A., Sonka, M., Hunninghake, G.W., McLennan, G.: Interstitial lung disease: a quantitative study using the adaptive multiple feature method. Am. J. Respir. Crit. Care Med. **159**(2), 519–525 (1999)

37. Vallières, M., Freeman, C.R., Skamene, S.R., El Naqa, I.: A radiomics model from joint FDG-PET and MRI texture features for the prediction of lung metastases in soft-tissue sarcomas of the extremities. Phys. Med. Biol. **60**(14), 5471 (2015)

38. Ye, F., Zhang, Z., Chakrabarty, K., Gu, X.: Board-level functional fault diagnosis using artificial neural networks, support-vector machines, and weighted-majority voting. IEEE Trans. Comput. Aided Des. Integr. Circuits Syst. **32**(5), 723–736 (2013)

NISAR Real Time Data Processing – A Simple and Futuristic View

Manavalan$^{(\boxtimes)}$

Centre for Development of Advanced Computing (C-DAC), Bangalore, India
manavalan@cdac.in, saimanaindia@gmail.com

Abstract. NASA – ISRO Synthetic Aperture Radar (NISAR) is an Interferometric synthetic aperture radar mission will be launched during 2021. NISAR will be the first radar imaging satellite to use dual frequency NASA L-band SAR and ISRO's S-band SAR payloads. In a day NISAR generates near to 85 TB of raw data and during its life time it generates more than 140 PB of data. Processing of any such Big Data is a tough task for standalone computers and servers. Moreover, SAR based application models should support in making available the critical processed results in real time or near real time mode. In line to this, a HPC based NISAR processing architecture that can meets the data processing and analyzing needs of NISAR like Big Data generating space missions is conceptualized and proposed. The proposed model is unique due to its support to the simultaneous processing of different frequency, polarization channels of SAR data as well as in virtually visualizing the end results. All together the proposed HPC-Big Data system will make available the simulation results within shortest possible time.

Keywords: NISAR · HPC · Big Data · System architecture

1 Introduction

Synthetic Aperture Radar (SAR) based earth imaging technology is becoming a most sought after earth imaging technology due to its strength in capturing the terrain information during all weather and round the clock periods as well as in capturing the earth surface both in high resolution spot mode and course resolution wide swath mode [1, 2]. Many countries are shifting considerable part of their space budget towards SAR based space imaging system due to its consistent reliability at critical occasions. With multiple advances happening in various fronts of Synthetic Aperture Radar (SAR) technology, as on date processing of any such high resolution multi frequency, multi polarization SAR signals and corresponding pre and post image processing operations requires, the support of using advanced HPC systems and related Big Data technologies as this can only make available the end results in near real time or real time mode [3, 4].

To be specific the NISAR (NASA-ISRO Synthetic Aperture Radar) mission which is a joint space mission of NASA and ISRO will be launched in the year 2021 is an dual frequency L- and S-band polarimetric SAR with 12-day interferometric orbit that will support systematic global coverage including cryosphere [5, 6]. As on date, projections

R. Patgiri et al. (Eds.): BigDML 2019, CCIS 1317, pp. 95–101, 2020.
https://doi.org/10.1007/978-3-030-62625-9_9

of NISAR satellite data acquisitions exhibits, that in a single day pass it can captures more than 85 Terabytes (TB) of earth observation data and during its life span of time this mission alone likely to generate 140 Petabytes (PB) of SAR raw data [7, 8]. Calibration of raw data and subsequent pre and post processing processes further generates TB to PB of SAR images. Similar situations likely to happen with many other future space borne missions as the respective SAR technology is already moving from space borne to air borne UAVSAR (Uninhabited Aerial Vehicle Synthetic Aperture Radar) mode which is already in use in many defense sectors of the world [9]. Overall, in future many such SAR systems generates TB to PB of data due to its multi frequency, multi-polarization capturing modes as well as due to the preference of generating high resolution spot mode images. Hence, processing of NISAR like Big Data will certainly become a challenge to many HPC cluster environment. The primary challenges includes:

- Storage of PBs of SAR raw data of each pass of satellite missions
- Temporal data indexing of routine satellite pass periods and in supporting specific data extraction of smaller terrain
- In supporting, the data download process of user specific data frames covering the region of interest or specific study area
- Computation involved in calibrating the source/raw radar signals to generate first level SAR data (Level 0B data)
- Pre and post processing of calibrated data as per the need and requirements of application specific research models
- Real Time or Near real time data processing of TBs of SAR data frames of critical locations is still a major challenge

To overcome many such challenges the data utilization of NISAR like dedicated SAR mission's has to be supported through distributed HPC storage and processing clusters. Any such setup that supports the real time/near real time processing require-ments of SAR specific application models helps in delivering the critical information within shortest possible time. The only thing expected from the application researcher group is that they have to fine tune and port their application models into such dedi-cated HPC clusters which is specially configured as per the processing requirements of NISAR like SAR system. Any model build over such dedicated or distributed cluster environment will be subsequently hardcoded as a routine service of respective applica-tion, mainly to support the temporal data processing of future requirements. In general, during regional scale disaster modelling when the amount of input data increases, the advantages of distributed HPC processing environment is quickly engrossed due to its scalable nature of providing the computing resources with reference to the input data size and other modelling requirements which altogether reduces the processing time. Such SAR processing systems on distributed environment is already well setup and supported by European Space Agency (ESA) through its Grid Processing on Demand (G-POD) environment where user move their specific simulations code or algorithms to the dedi-cated cluster of G-POD and then relate the source data that resides in respective G-POD clusters [10, 11]. Similar system supporting SAR data processing was also prototyped with India's first Grid Computing environment Grid GARUDA [12] which is currently non-operational.

In line to above detailed distributed SAR data processing systems, this article mainly discusses the core design perspectives of a HPC based system architecture that supports both real time as well as offline data processing of NISAR like SAR missions. Emphasis has been given in evolving a Big Data based HPC system which can handle TB of input SAR data processing of same geographical region of different frequency, polarization and disseminates the processed end results through remote visualization techniques. Any such operational setup supports the researchers as well as end users to visualize the geographical or terrain signature content of SAR images of his area of interest simultaneously at different frequencies, polarization channels [13]. Due to this simultaneous processing of different frequencies, different polarization channels of SAR system this article differs from existing HPC based Grid/cluster environment. The proposed architecture of the NISAR data processing system is detailed in the following section.

2 Architecture

The architecture of proposed SAR SLC data processing system which support simultaneous processing of NISAR data is shown in Fig. 1. The efforts involved in RADAR signal processing and subsequent SAR raw data to SLC data (Single Look Complex) processing of the NISAR data is out of the scope of this article as emphasis has been given in evolving an HPC architecture that can suit for the simultaneous processing of NISAR SLC data of different frequencies and polarizations. Hence, as shown in Fig. 1, it has been assumed that SAR raw data and corresponding SLC data of same geographical region resides in Storage Cluster-I which shares input SLC data for the next level processing.

From storage cluster-I, the SLC data of L- and S-band SAR of same geographical regions is transferred to two different computing clusters where the first one will be processing the L-band SLC data and the second one supports processing of S-band SLC data. Depending upon the multi-look calibration factor (1:4; 2:8 and 3:16), which is mainly decided by the SAR data processing scientist with reference to the end user application specific requirements, the master node of individual L-and S- band computing cluster allocates the no of slave nodes as shown in Fig. 1. For example when 1:4 and 2:8 multi-look parameter is hardcoded as part of the programming paradigm only two slave processing nodes for each L- and S-band clusters will be activated. When the user further interested to compare the output of 3:16 multi-look image additional slave processing node will be activated. Subsequent to this, the respective SLC data preferably has to be copied to each slave node or communication between the slave node and master node has to be maintained all the time by which the slave nodes can read the source SLC data that has been placed in master node. In the first option, the data is processed within short period of duration as the input SLC data is copied to each computing slave node whereas the second option consumes considerable processing time as communication between master and slave node has to be maintained to support constant read and write process which becomes a memory intensive model. Hence, with reference to meeting the real time requirement, simultaneous transfer of source SLC data to compute node i.e. slave nodes has to be automated through a workflow environment. At the end of this process

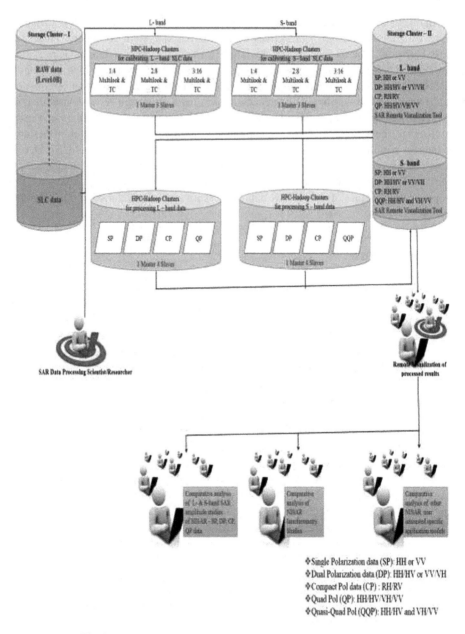

Fig. 1. Architecture of NISAR SLC SAR data processing system

multi-looked terrain corrected SAR images are generated and same is transferred to the Storage Cluster-II where L- and S-band SAR images will be indexed in corresponding storage nodes. Following such intermediate processes helps the user to retrieve the processed SAR image of different multi-looked data straight from the Storage Cluster-II without performing any SLC data calibration process which is a time consuming task. To support terrain correction process it is mandatory the user has to relate the accurate DEM of the respective region or need to use open source DEM [14].

To continue the next level processing, as shown in Fig. 1 the different polarization SAR images (SP, DP, CP and QP) of L- and S-band frequency has to be shared to two different computing clusters as one supports the L-band data processing and the other one supports S-band data processing. By this, the L-band Cluster will be supporting Single Polarization (SP) - HH or VV; Dual Polarization (DP) - HH/HV or VV/VH; Compact Pol (CP) - RH/RV and Quad Pol (QP) - HH/HV/VH/VV data processing whereas in the case of S-band Quasi-Quad Pol data (QQP) - HH/HV and VH/VV replaces the Quad Pol data of its counterpart. In such case, each individual computing cluster transfers one single polarization image from an individual computing node by which four slave nodes has to be allotted to process all the polarization channels of L- and S-band SAR images. In parallel to this, it is expected the application model which has to extract the end user specific information from each individual polarization SAR channels will be compiled in each slave nodes and respective simulation is executed immediately after receiving the multi-looked image from Storage Cluster-II. To meet this purpose another automated workflow environment which can copy the multi-look data to the different slave nodes as well as monitor the respective data transfer and compute process has to be developed and deployed at master node level. In addition to above data processing methods, it is also possible to allocate the individual slave nodes to process the individual polarization image such as HH, VV, HH/HV, VV/VH, RH/RV, HH/HV, VH/VV along with the application model that has to be ported to each slave node. This is not addressed in this article as well as reflected in Fig. 1 mainly to maintain the simplicity of the proposed architecture.

Once the application simulation is completed at slave computing nodes the results are transferred back to the Storage Cluster-II and indexed against corresponding L- and S-band storage nodes. A SAR visualization tool which supports remote visualization of individual SAR images and corresponding results has to be installed in each L- and S-band storage nodes. To support remote visualization the X-11 forwarding has to be suitably configured at Storage Cluster-II nodes as well as to the remote system of the end-user with a stipulated time frame. This will support the end user in simultaneously viewing and comparing the results of his application that has been derived using different frequency, polarization SAR channels. At the end of the process completion, simultaneous remote visualization and its analysis, end users will certainly bring out many significant insights of the application as the data of same geographical region of different frequencies, polarizations has been derived, compared and analyzed in the same time [14].

3 Conclusion

As on date there is no single distributed SAR processing environment is proposed that can support the simultaneous processing of different frequency, polarization data where the end user will be able to visualize and compare the processed results of their area of interest of same geographical region. Setting up the proposed NISAR processing system can meet such expectations by which it will become a significant HPC-Big Data platform for worldwide researchers who can build specific application models in the fields of - Natural Ecosystem studies such as River linking, Agriculture Biomass estimation, Crop monitoring, Forest mapping and Biomass estimation, Mangroves-Wetlands mapping; Land Surface Deformation studies such as Inter and Co-seismic deformation studies, Land Subsidence, Landslides and Volcanic deformation studies; Cryosphere studies covering Polar Ice Shelf monitoring & estimation, Sea Ice dynamics, Glacier dynamics of Himalayan region, Mountain Snow-Glacier relationship studies; Coastal Studies & Oceanography which includes Coastal erosion, shoreline dynamics, High and Low Tide lines mapping, Bathymetry studies, Ocean surface wind dynamics, Ocean wave spectra, Ship detection; Disaster Response studies covering Floods, Forest Fire, Oil Spill, Earthquakes as well as analyzing the impact of any other man induced disasters; Geological applications such as Structural & Lithological mapping, Lineament study, Paleo-Channel study, Geomorphological mapping, etc.

To be specific NISAR mission during its lifespan likely to generate 140 PB of raw data which in turn will generates same amount of additional data during its pre, post processing levels as well as during various application specific simulations as mentioned above. For any application, even for a small scale terrain data of such nature cannot be handled as well as processed by high end standalone computers or servers. In such case setting up the proposed HPC-Big Data SAR data processing platform will become a timely solution. To completely absorb the advantages of such distributed processing environment the application scientists also need to find tune and enable their application models as part of the proposed system as this meets the expectations of real time simulations where the end results from different frequency and polarization SAR channels can be derived within shortest possible time and compared.

References

1. Manavalan, R.: SAR image analysis techniques for flood area mapping - literature survey. Earth Sci. Inf. **10**(1), 1–14 (2016). https://doi.org/10.1007/s12145-016-0274-2
2. Manavalan, R.: Review article, Review of synthetic aperture radar frequency, polarization, and incidence angle data for mapping the inundated regions. Int. J. Appl. Remote Sensing **12**(2), 021501 (2018). https://doi.org/10.1117/1.JRS.12.021501
3. Lanari, R (2015) From ERS-1 TO SENTINEL-1, A big data challenge for 25 years of DInSAR observations. Proceedings of IEEE International Geoscience and Remote Sensing Symposium, Milan, pp. 1460–1463. https://doi.org/10.1109/igarss.2015.7326054
4. Elefante, S., Zinno, I., De Luca, C., Manunta, M., Lanari, R., Casu, F.: Big DInSAR data processing through the P-SBAS algorithm. In: IEEE International Geoscience and Remote Sensing Symposium, Milan, pp. 2696–2698 (2015). https://doi.org/10.1109/igarss.2015.7326369
5. Rosen, P.A, Hensley, S., Shaffer, S., Veilleux, L., RajuSagi, V., Satish, R.: The NASA-ISRO SAR mission - An international space partnership for science and societal benefit. In: IEEE Radar Conference, Arlington, VA, pp. 1610–1613 (2015). https://doi.org/10.1109/radar.2015.7131255
6. Xaypraseuth, P., Satish, R., Chatterjee, A.: NISAR spacecraft concept overview: design challenges for a proposed flagship dual-frequency SAR mission. In: IEEE Aerospace Conference, Big Sky, MT, pp. 1–11 (2015). https://doi.org/10.1109/aero.2015.7118935

7. Earth Science Data Systems (ESDS) Program. https://earthdata.nasa.gov/getting-ready-for nisar

8. Blumenfeld, J.: Getting Ready for NISAR – and for Managing Big Data using the Commercial Cloud, 17 April 2019. Accessed on 12 Oct 2019

9. Uninhabited Aerial Vehicle Synthetic Aperture Radar (UAVSAR), NASA-JPL. 22 January 2019. https://uavsar.jpl.nasa.gov. Accessed 12 Oct 2019

10. ESA Grid Processing on Demand. https://gpod.eo.esa.int/. Accessed 12 Oct 2019

11. De Luca, C., et al.: Unsupervised on-demand web service for DInSAR processing: The P-SBAS implementation within the ESA G-POD environment. In: IEEE International Geoscience and Remote Sensing Symposium, Milan, pp 2692–2695 (2015). https://doi.org/10.1109/igarss.2015.7326368

12. Grid Computing, Centre for Development of Advanced Computing. https://www.cdac.in/index.aspx?id=grid_comp. Accessed 12 Oct 2019

13. Manavalan, R., Rao, Y.S., Krishna Mohan, B.: Comparative flood area analysis of C- band VH, VV and L-band HH polarizations SAR data. Int. J. Remote Sens. **38**(16), 4645–4654 (2017). https://doi.org/10.1080/01431161.2017.1325534

14. Manavalan, R., Rao, Y.S.: DEM and SAR image based flood feature extraction tech- niques to map the deep and shallow flood inundated regions of known as well as remote disaster regions. Geocarto Int. **29**(7), 745–757 (2013). https://doi.org/10.1080/10106049.2013.838310

Author Index

Printed in the United States
By Bookmasters